Many Roads Lead Eastward

accessible
hospitable
passable
enjoyable
habitable

Many Roads Lead Eastward

Overtures to Catholic Biblical Theology

Robert D. Miller II, OFS

CASCADE *Books* • Eugene, Oregon

MANY ROADS LEAD EASTWARD
Overtures to Catholic Biblical Theology

Cascade Books
An Imprint of Wipf and Stock Publishers
199 W. 8th Ave., Suite 3
Eugene, OR 97401

www.wipfandstock.com

paperback ISBN 13: 978-1-4982-8471-4
hardcover ISBN: 978-1-4982-8471-4
ebook ISBN: 978-1-4982-8472-1

Cataloging-in-Publication data:

Names: Miller, Robert D., II.

Title: Many roads lead eastward : overtures to Catholical biblical theology / Robert D. Miller II.

Description: Eugene, OR: Cascade Books. | Includes bibliographical references. and index

Identifiers: 978-1-4982-8471-4 (paperback) | 978-1-4982-8471-4 (hardcover) | 978-1-4982-8472-1 (ebook)

Subjects: LCSH: Bible—Theology. | Bible—Study and teaching—Catholic Church.

Classification: BS587 M55 2016 (print). | BS587 (ebook)

Manufactured in the USA

Nihil Obstat:
Rev. Christopher Begg, S.T.D., Ph.D.
Censor Deputatus

Imprimatur:
Most Rev. Barry C. Knestout
Auxiliary Bishop of Washington
Archdiocese of Washington
January 20, 2016

Contents

Models of Revelation (handwritten)

Preface

This book is the product of decades of thought and conversation about the topics it treats. The issues discussed first challenged me in a graduate course on "Sources of Christian Doctrine" in 1991 that I took with John T. Ford, who is now my colleague at the Catholic University of America. John first introduced me to Karl Bühler and to Avery Dulles's *Models of Revelation,* which are the framework of this study. Incipient forms of this study were presented at Duke Divinity School and the Pontifical College Josephinum in the early years of this century. The general contents of the book became courses I taught, first to seminarians at Mount St. Mary's Seminary and finally, in 2013, to doctoral students at Catholic University. The insights of all of those students have been valuable, but I could not have written what I have without the students in the 2013 Old Testament Theology seminar, who therefore deserve be mentioned by name: Nathanael Polinski, O.S.B., John Robert Skeldon, Katherine Brown, Adam Tune, Sung Cho, Maria Rodriguez, and Brian Main. I have also benefited greatly from discussions with several scholars on the LuxVerbi listserv devoted to the Bible and theology. I thank graduate students Allison Ralph and Eric Trinka for their editorial assistance.

In spite of the decades-long gestation of this book and post-2014 editorial work, the birth took largely one weekend in early 2014. I am immensely grateful to my wife, Anne-Marie, for sending me away for a weekend to write, and to our friends Ed and

Kathy for the use of their beach house in which to do so. The reason for writing this book is encapsulated in its last paragraph. I hope that readers will find it enriching as well as informative.

Abbreviations

ABD	*Anchor Bible Dictionary*
BibInt	*Biblical Interpretation*
BibIntSer	Biblical Interpretation Series
BTB	*Biblical Theology Bulletin*
CBQ	*Catholic Biblical Quarterly*
ExAud	*Ex Auditu*
ExpTim	*Expository Times*
FAT	*Forschungen zum Alten Testament*
IJST	*International Journal of Systematic Theology*
Int	*Interpretation*
ITQ	*Irish Theological Quarterly*
JAAR	*Journal of the American Academy of Religion*
JBL	*Journal of Biblical Literature*
JR	*Journal of Religion*
JSOT	*Journal of the Study of the Old Testament*
JSNT	*Journal of the Study of the New Testament*

JTI	*Journal of Theological Interpretation*
LHBOTS	Library of Hebrew Bible/Old Testament Studies
NRTh	*La nouvelle revue théologique*
OTL	Old Testament Library
QD	Quaestiones Disputatae
RelSRev	*Religious Studies Review*
SBLSP	*Society of Biblical Literature Seminar Papers*
SJT	*Scottish Journal of Theology*
ST	*Studia Theologica*
StZ	*Stimmen der Zeit*
TQ	*Theologische Quartalschrift*
ThSt	Theologisiche Studiën
ThTo	*Theology Today*
TS	*Theological Studies*
TTZ	*Trierer theologische Zeitschrift*

1

The Great Divide

INTRODUCTION

Perhaps at no time since the 1960s has the world of biblical scholarship been so awash with works of "Biblical Theology" and "Theological Interpretation."[1] What was, for a time and at least in many circles, taboo has become once again *au currant.* This sort of thing is not what this book is about.

When biblical theology elucidates major themes, themes such as covenant, grace, people of God, and prophetic witness, it does so ordinarily on its own terms, unpacking for the reader in homiletic style, albeit more academic-sounding, what exegesis has discovered. With regard to "theology," this at most leaves room for a dialogue. The exegete has something to say on a theological topic; the systematic theologian (or moral theologian or the like) has something else to say on the same subject. Together, this ought to benefit the Church. That is not what this book is about.

The Second Vatican Council's Constitution on Divine Revelation, *Dei Verbum,* says in paragraph 24 that the study of Sacred

---

1. Among others, Treier, *Theological Interpretation of Scripture*; Green, *Practicing Theological Interpretation*; Green and Tim Meadowcraft, eds., *Ears That Hear*; Sarisky, *Scriptural Interpretation.*

Scripture must be the soul of theology. This idiom, *velute anima sacra theologiae*, is borrowed from Leo XIII's *Providentissimus Deus*. This phrase does not mean that exegesis is a dialogue partner with theology, the practice now increasingly common. Nor does it mean that the Bible is to be the basis of theological research and practice, as if every good book on soteriology or medical ethics ought to begin with a chapter on the Bible, or every seminary course on grace or sacraments begin with an opening session on the "biblical material"—practices not altogether rare nor at all wrong in themselves. In fact, such practices are enjoined upon theologians in many other documents. *Optatum totius* 16 asks that moral theology be "nourished more on the teaching of the Bible" (it is not clear what exactly it is to be "more" [*magis*] than, but presumably "more" than moral theology of the casuistic manuals of 1900–1960). Benedict XVI, in *Verbum Domini* 35, stated that, "Where theology is not essentially the interpretation of the Church's Scripture, such a theology no longer has a foundation."[2] *Dei Verbum*, however, says that the *study* of Sacred Scripture must be the soul of theology. This means that it is not the Bible but exegesis that should ground academic theology. The systematic theologians are not the ones expected to engage in this study, as if every doctoral degree in political theology ought to require a masters in biblical studies as a prerequisite and every liturgist ought to gain fluency in Ugaritic and Akkadian, or even Hebrew.[3] Nor are the exegetes expected to be doing the theology, a practice far more tempting and far more common. It is not for the Hebrew Bible scholar to make statements about prevenient grace. But a simple dialogue will not work. The "soul of theology" metaphor works in one direction. The study of Scripture takes place first, and the results of that study then form the *sine qua non* foundation of academic theology. And it is this, in spite of the surfeit of books on theological interpretation, that remains sorely missing.[4]

2. Cf. also Paul VI, "Address to the PBC," 8.

3. Karl Rahner noted the impossibility of leaving the entire task to the theologians; "Exegesis and Dogmatic Theology," 71–72.

4. Abraham, "Authority of Scripture."

Other theologians and biblical scholars have observed this impasse: serious scholarly work on the Bible seems to be of little use to practicing theologians. Some are sure it is the fault of the notorious historical-critical method. The opening volley in this challenge was probably an often-reprinted 1980 article in *Theology Today* by David Steinmetz of Duke Divinity School titled "The Superiority of Pre-Critical Exegesis."[5] A 2000 article in *Homiletics and Pastoral Review* dismissed the historical-critical method as "conjectures which, in general, have no or little pastoral application—and yet months of [seminary] class time are often spent jumping from one such hypothesis to another."[6] Even theologians such as Augustine DiNoia have concluded that the method has had considerable negative impact on all areas of the Church's life.[7]

ORIGINS OF THE IMPASSE

The intellectual heritage of the historical-critical method is much debated. Scott Hahn, Benjamin Wiker, and Raúl Kerbs maintain that its founding fathers are Baruch Spinoza and Thomas Hobbes and the rise of rationalism.[8] But there is no reason to attribute the rise of the historical-critical method to atheistic Enlightenment philosophies.[9] If we start in recent centuries, with the Old Testament methodology of the famous Julius Wellhausen (1844–1918), often presented as both the author of the Documentary Hypothesis and the methods of source criticism, although he followed many others in both,[10] we will find his work driven by his theology.[11] His

5. Steinmetz, "Superiority of Pre-critical Exegesis."

6. Bush, "*Sola Scriptura*," 32.

7. DiNoia and Mulcahy, "Scripture in Sacramental Theology," 336; also Kelly, "A Wayward Turn."

8. Hahn and Wiker, *Politicizing the Bible*; Kerbs, "Método Histórico."

9. So also Morrow, "Politics of Biblical Interpretation"; and Tilley, "The Birth of Ideology."

10. Wellhausen, *Prolegomena*, 13.

11. Bright, *Early Israel*, 22; Hayes, "Wellhausen as a Historian," 55; Rendtorff, "The Paradigm is Changing," 2–3.

sources for the Pentateuch, although derived by source criticism, were put in a sequence according to the overall progress of history as the Protestant dogmatic system defined it.[12] Wellhausen was not alone in this sort of theologically-driven higher criticism. Luke Timothy Johnson notes that the establishment of the historical-critical method in the nineteenth century "combined scientific historiography with specifically Lutheran theological premises."[13]

John Barton has argued that the origins of the historical-critical method are considerably earlier and far different. He traces higher criticism to the Renaissance and its "return to the sources,"[14] particularly to the Christian Humanism of Erasmus and the Catholic "Counter-" Reformation that grew from it. It was the understanding of Tradition propounded by the Council of Trent (1545–63) taken as an analogy for the development of the Old Testament that gave rise to source and redaction and traditions criticisms as we now have them.[15] Far from being an organized attack on Catholicism, biblical criticism "had, indeed, a consciously anti-Protestant intention."[16] Catholic apologists argued, "The church could never be content with *sola scriptura*" if the Bible itself was a product of sources, tradents, and redactors.[17]

In fact, says Barton, higher criticism is older than that. It derives from Aristotle's *Poetics*, and is visible in Jerome (esp. *De viris illustribus*) and in the patristic School of Antioch.[18] Barton is aware that claims that the Fathers of Antioch (Theodoret of Cyr, Theodore of Mopsuestia, John Chrysostom) were "literal," "historical" readers of Scripture have been exaggerated.[19] But these Church

tradent – one responsible for preserving, handing on oral tradition

12. Wellhausen, *Prolegomena*, xiii, 12. For discussion, see Moore and Sherwood, "Biblical Studies 'after' Theory," 101 and 101–2 n30.

13. Johnson, "Catholic Biblical Scholarship," 15 n16, 21.

14. Barton, *Nature of Biblical Criticism*, 7, 124.

15. Ibid., 125.

16. Ibid., 126.

17. Ibid.

18. Ibid., 130–32.

19. O'Keefe, "Rejecting One's Masters."

Fathers are real biblical critics as readers of genre,[20] the students
of Libanius (fourth-century Nicomedian rhetorician) who are
looking for *akolouthia* (narrative structure). While Libanius was
teacher to Chrysostom, he was also the mentor of Basil the Great
and Gregory Nazianzus. For Gregory, what Barton will call the
"Plain Sense"—"A semantic or linguistic and a literary operation
first and foremost, only indirectly concerned with the original,
the historical, or the literal meaning"[21]—was the key to the divine
author's intended meaning. Perhaps these patristic and Tridentine
origins are why, according to the Anglican Barton, "The Catholic
Church . . . has now embraced critical approaches perhaps more
wholeheartedly than any other Christian confession."[22]

Hitherto, the terms "higher criticism," "historical-critical
method," and "plain sense" have been used interchangeably and
without explicit definition. Let us provide a bottom-line definition
for the historical-critical method. For the Bible to be understood,
this method holds, it has to be seen within its historical *Sitz im
Leben*, within the larger context of ancient Near Eastern culture
as determined by archaeological discovery and the tradition of
comparative philology.[23] This definition does not require the historical critic to work in an atheistic rationalism.[24] Certainly, the
twentieth-century paradigm, W. F. Albright, did not, and in fact,
he "raised biblical history to a pinnacle of religious significance."[25]
Nevertheless, what mattered was the history. "The landslide of text
and artifacts found in the ancient Near East in the last two centuries enticed the field into a confident positivistic attitude toward
finding and recovering the historical and comparing it with Israel's
ancient texts."[26] Nevertheless, as John Collins writes, "Historical

20. Barton, *Nature*, 132, 134, 189.

21. Ibid., 101.

22. Ibid., 141.

23. Machinist, "William Foxwell Albright," 392.

24. As maintained by Daley, "Patristic Exegesis"; DiNoia and Mulcahy,
"Scripture and Sacramental Theology," 337.

25. Kutsko, "History as Liturgy."

26. Kutsko, "History"; Smith, "Monotheistic Re–Readings."

criticism, properly understood, does not claim that the original historical context exhausts the meaning of a text."[27]

Yet, as Patricia McDonald has observed, "gains in biblical understanding, although of intrinsic interest to scholars, have often turned out to be scant fare for sustaining the life of the religious communities to which those scholars belong."[28] Herein lays the impasse. It has two sides. If theologians are unable to utilize exegesis produced today, and "the 'so what?' question is prominent,"[29] it is the fault of both the exegetes and the theologians.

Theologians of the Post-Tridentine Church all the way up to the conservative neo-Scholastics Joseph Kleutgen, Louis Billot, and Ambroise Gardeil in the nineteenth century had been content to use Scripture to provide "a set of predictable proof-texts for theological positions."[30] In the first half of the twentieth century, however, there was a promising "definite shift of theological . . . interests toward the Bible."[31] One of the main characteristics of the *nouvelle théologie* was its basis in the biblical renewal. In the 1950s and 1960s "there were Catholic theologians and exegetes who tried hard to find a grounding for Catholic exegesis in a clearer understanding of inspiration, canonicity, hermeneutics, and the patristic heritage."[32] Pierre Benoit and Luis Alonso Schökel stand out among them.

"Yet, on the whole, their work was largely bypassed . . . , particularly in the United States, because the American . . . systematic theologians were so focused on the relatively unbiblical systems of Rahner and Lonergan."[33] Meanwhile in Europe, *nouvelle théologie's ressourcement* of the Church Fathers led theologians like Yves Congar, Louis Bouyer, Henri de Lubac, and others to a figural exegesis

---

27. Collins, *Encounters with Biblical Theology*, 2.

28. McDonald, "Biblical Scholarship," 127.

29. Ibid., 128.

30. Johnson, "Catholic Biblical Scholarship," 7.

31. Farkasfalvy, "Case for Spiritual Exegesis," 332.

32. McDonald, "Biblical Scholarship," 128.

33. Ibid.; cf. Ratzinger, "Biblical Interpretation in Crisis," 3. For examples, see Rahner, *Grundkurs des Glaubens*, 28.

that biblical scholars were explicitly rejecting.[34] Dialogue was effectively closed. Over the course of the last century, theology as a whole developed less interest in the Bible, as it "sought to pursue its own necessary agenda, often in a more contemporary contextual setting."[35] By late century, theology showed little interest "in absorbing, digesting and integrating the vast amount of biblical learning."[36] J. Richard Middleton points out that, "the writings of systematic theologians simply ignore the massive literature in Old Testament scholarship."[37] Moral theology was no different.[38] Once convinced by Joseph Fletcher that Scripture could replace Natural Law as a primary source only with difficulty,[39] ethicists used *Gaudium et Spes*, 4, 11, and *Lumen Gentium* 2 as justification for making the "signs of the times" and the *sensus fidelium* the main sources for moral theology.[40] The few opponents of this sort of moral theology, heirs of mid-century Thomistic theologians Marie-Michel Labourdette, Pietro Parente, and their reaction to *Nouvelle Théologie*—which never went "back to the Bible" in the first place, today emphasize Aristotle and the Thomism of the 1950s overlaid with John Paul II's anthropology.

On the other hand, exegetes show little interest in a theological appropriation of their work. Again, there were some mid-century overtures: Raymond Brown hoped his *Introduction to the New Testament* would have a positive *pastoral* effect for the church and future Catholic leaders.[41] Yet, as Patricia McDonald explains:

> The specialization within the exegetical enterprise leaves exegetes unable to engage with the fundamental theological questions underlying the place of the Bible in Christian life . . . Younger biblical scholars are much

34. Daley, "*La Nouvelle Théologie.*"

35. Dempsey and Loewe, "Introduction," xi–xv, xi.

36. Farkasfalvy, "Case for Spiritual Exegesis," 334.

37. Middleton, *The Liberating Image*, 24.

38. Harrington and Keenan, *Jesus and Virtue Ethics*, 13.

39. Fletcher, *Situation Ethics*.

40. Dulles, "Theology in Priestly Formation."

41. Kurz "Response to Luke Johnson," 146.

> less likely to be ordained men who belong to a residential religious community. So . . . their experience is less likely to include an extended education in philosophical and theological disciplines that is integrated into the community's apostolate and the Church's liturgical life and structures . . . In consequence, an exegete's conversation partners are much more likely to be scholars from other Christian denominations or from the secular academy than the theologians from his or her own tradition.[42]

Luke Timothy Johnson came to the same conclusion.[43] It is odd that DiNoia and Mulcahy believe that "very few people would pursue careers in non-theological exegesis if they could only study questions essentially irrelevant to the Bible as Scripture ('what does the Bible tell us about Antiochus Epiphanes?'). Because, in fact, most people who study the Bible are interested in it precisely because it is received by believers as divine revelation."[44] The latter statement is simply wrong, as many nonbelievers populate the ranks of the biblical academy, and the Antiochus example is exactly the sort of research most biblical scholars do. The 2008 XII Bishops' Synod on "The Word of God in the Life and Mission of the Church" rightly wrote in its *Propositiones*, "An unproductive separation exists between exegesis and theology even at the highest academic levels" (no. 27).

THE NECESSITY OF HERMENEUTICS

For reasons I have already outlined at the start of this book, some may object that the gap between exegesis and theology has already begun to be bridged. It cannot be disputed that some biblical interpretation is engaged in conversation with faith communities in the context of the world at large. My contention, however, is that this

---

42. McDonald, "Biblical Scholarship," 129; Cf. Farkasfalvy, "Case for Spiritual Exegesis," 336.

43. Johnson, "What's Catholic," 12–13.

44. DiNoia and Mulcahy, "Scripture in Sacramental Theology," 343.

is merely *Wissenschaft* plus pious reflection or *parenesis*.[45] When the aim is to "recover from scripture 'valuable theological insights' that may have relevance for today,"[46] or, conversely, "how our lives . . . might fitly answer to that narration and participate in the truth that [the text] tells,"[47] that is homiletics, not hermeneutics.

The renewed interest since the 1990s in what the text *means*, not only "meant," in its relevance for faith, is laudable. But although biblical scholars of the 1950s and 1960s regularly published discussions of the nature of revelation, those of the 21st century have no experience over the preceding decades with hermeneutics and so began to do theological interpretation without any theory. And as K. H. Miskotte wrote, "Exegesis is only scientifically responsible if one lets oneself be led by a thoughtful hermeneutic."[48] The scholar's hermeneutic is determined by what they see as the ultimate reference of theological language, but also—and this will be the focus of this book—by how they see revelation mediated.

Without hermeneutics, biblical scholars are apt to disparage any mention of inspiration or revelation with comments like "there is a lot in that Bible that's not revelatory of *my* God."[49] Theologians, too, "avoid the enormous conceptual confusions and redherrings attendant to, say, 'revelation.'"[50] With good hermeneutics, however, God can be immoral in the Bible and it still be inspired and revelation.[51]

45. Similar conclusions are reached by DiNoia and Mulcahy, "Scripture in Sacramental Theology," 343–44.

46. Dempsey and Loewe, "Introduction," xiii. We should not be deceived: patristic exegesis was by no means mere "homiletic application" of the text; Daley, "Is Patristic," 201.

47. Hays, *Moral Vision*, 298–99.

48. Miskotte, *Zur biblischen Hermeneutik*, 4.

49. The remark was made at the 2004 meeting of the College Theology Society, Washington, DC. On the Kantian roots of such sentiments, see Moore and Sherwood, "Biblical Studies," 98, 106.

50. Kelsey, "Theological Use of Scripture," 181–88.

51. I refer here to a sophisticated hermeneutic, not merely "a hermeneutic of receptive trust, even as we use suspicion toward sinful interpreters"; Billings, *Word of God*, 132. We must grapple with problem texts, not gloss them over or excise them.

The great Carmelite Old Testament scholar, Roland Murphy defined the biblical theology he sought as "construal or synthesis of biblical data concerning God, man, and nature in biblical categories."[52] However, realizing that the biblical "data" were contradictory and unconstruable (cf. *Verbum Domini*, 39), and that "there is no single biblical theology as a literary unit,"[53] he settled, as have many others, for theologically oriented exegesis. At its best, this becomes the project Dempsey and Loewe propose, "both disciplines [Bible and theology] making a joint contribution to the fields of liturgical-pastoral theology [and] spirituality,"[54] which is not the same as exegetes producing something of use to systematicians. At its worse, there are examples where source criticism is used to find a more primitive, inclusive composition that can be made normative when disabused of its "orthodox" accretions.[55] It is done as Mark Smith describes:

> when scholars working in archaeology, biblical studies, or history of religion write explicitly or implicitly about Judaism and Christianity for audiences including Jews and Christians, their intellectual enterprise sometimes includes the unstated task of offering an alternative theology melding theology and nontheological data anchored in the culturally prestigious discourses of history and archaeology—in short, a Bible and a theology without religious experience or even belief.[56]

There is an additional problem. Catholicism views the Church Fathers as the privileged interpreters of Scripture (*Interpretation of the Bible in the Church*, III.B.5). The Congregation for the Clergy's 1999, *The Priest and the Third Christian Millennium*, states: "The Fathers of the Church . . . teach us how to penetrate the meaning

52. Murphy, "When is Theology Biblical?"
53. Ibid., contra House, "God's Design and Postmodernism," 33.
54. Dempsey and Loewe, "Introduction," xi.
55. See Osiek, "Family in Early Christianity."
56. Smith, "Monotheistic Re-readings," 31; the same phenomenon is described by Ratzinger, "Biblical Interpretation," 2; Johnson, "Catholic Biblical Scholarship," 18.

What about 21st century, ♀, multicultural lens

of the revealed Word." On first blush, most patristic exegesis, thoroughly imbued with figural readings, seems a difficult thing to appropriate today.[57]

We are not called to reduplicate their methods, however, although some have tried,[58] but to emulate their overall designs, as *Verbum Domini*, no. 37 makes clear. On a certain level, I would argue that we are emulating them precisely by following the historical-critical method, for the following reason. The Fathers of Alexandria, for example, did not engage in speculative allegorical readings because it looked like fun. They did so because the intellectual climate of Alexandria was thoroughly Neo-Platonist, where even the Jewish philosopher Philo had been allegorizing the Torah in precisely the same way. They were enculturating the Gospel into their world.[59] That is, what John Paul II called "the incarnation of the Gospel in native cultures and also the introduction of these cultures into the life of the Church" (*Slavorum Apostoli*, 21). The School of Antioch opposed allegory for the same reason: their intellectual culture consisted of non-Hellenistic Syrian Judaism or Hellenistic philosophy that was not that of Platonic allegorists but the rhetoric of the Stoics and "wisdom as a source of freedom" of the Cynics, Diogenes, and Solon. Therefore, would we not be enculturating in *our* intellectual culture by using the historical-critical method "to help its members to understand better the whole of the Christian mystery?" (John Paul II, *Catechesi Tradendae*, 33; cf. *Familiaris Consortio*, 10; *CCC* 1232).

Nevertheless, I will readily admit that much historical-critical scholarship on its own does *not* emulate the overall designs of patristic exegesis.[60] Most scholars do not "approach individual passages against the assumed background of a single story of God's

57. Breck, "Vérité et Sens," 2–3.

58. This is the error of the Roman Theological Forum (www.rtforum.org), and, e.g., McCambly, "Song of Songs."

59. Jackson has shown this quite clearly in her analysis of Cyril of Jerusalem, "Cyril of Jerusalem."

60. McDonald, "Biblical Scholarship," 126.

work in the world"[61] or view Christ as the hermeneutical key to all of Scripture.[62] It is not the intent of many to seek a meaning that addresses our spiritual health, soaked in and shaped by the Gospel within the Church's reflection and devotion and worship,[63] or to be a means by which the Scriptures will bring about the divine life in other Christians.[64]

THE NECESSITY OF THE HISTORICAL-CRITICAL METHOD

For the past several decades, many have argued that rather than making Scripture the "soul of theology," the historical-critical method "had the effect of further eroding the coherence of the biblical revelation by fragmenting the Bible into competing historical shards. The Priestly writer and Paul compete for control of the meaning of Genesis. Isaiah is beaten back from the New Testament to his exilic context."[65] The ultimate indictment of the method was probably the Mariologist René Laurentin, who referred to it as the "excrement of historical research."[66]

Others maintained that the historical-critical methods are driven by an "accursed spirit of pride, presumption, and superficiality, disguised under minute investigations and hypocritical literal exactness."[67] Yet this latter quote is not from a present-day critic of the method, but from the inflammatory pamphlet by Dolindo Ruotolo that was sent to Italian bishops in the 1940s and which provoked Pius XII's encyclical *Divino afflante Spiritu* in response. Ruotolo proposed as an alternative a revival of patristic exegesis,

61. Daley, "Patristic Exegesis," 194–95, cf. 198.

62. Ibid. 195; Anatolios, "Experience of Reading Scripture," 363.

63. Anatolios, "Experience of Reading Scripture," 361; Daley, "Patristic Exegesis," 200.

64. Anatolios, "Experience of Reading Scripture," 361, 369; Daley, "Patristic Exegesis," 201.

65. O'Keefe, "Rejecting One's Masters," 244.

66. Laurentin, *Evangiles de l'Enfance*, 439.

67. "Dain Cohenel" [Dolindo Ruotolo], "Un gravissimo pericolo," 40.

producing a ten thousand-page commentary,[68] which was placed on the *Index of Forbidden Books* by a decree of the Holy Office.[69]

Catholic biblical scholars cannot solve the problem by rejecting the historical-critical method.[70] *Dei Verbum* rightly "attained the right of domicile for historical interpretation within the Church," as Walter Kasper put it.[71] Benedict XI said of *Dei Verbum*, "the text binds together loyalty to Church tradition with the yes to critical science."[72] And John Paul II: "*Dei Verbum* . . . served to silence the sharply polemical attacks made against these exegetical methods at the beginning of the Council."[73] *Verbum Domini* (32) affirms, "Before all else, we need to acknowledge the benefits that historical-critical exegesis and other recently-developed methods of textual analysis have brought to the Church. For the Catholic understanding of sacred Scripture, attention to such methods is indispensable." I cannot agree with those who say, as one author has, that the method itself is "dangerous to a theological enterprise because by equating the human author's intended meaning with the "True" meaning, it fails to recognize the divine authorship of the text."[74] It is *by* seeking the "meaning the sacred writer intended" (*Dei Verbum* 12) that Catholic biblical interpretation approaches the divine author's intent.[75]

Inspiration, like Christology, is incarnational (*Dei Verbum* 13)—an analogy we shall promote in more detail in chapter 2.[76] The Fathers of the Church were fond of comparing the divine and

68. Dolino Ruotolo, *La Sacra Scrittura*.

69. Dated November 20, 1940.

70. As per Reno, "Biblical Theology."

71. Kasper, "'*Dei Verbum* Audiens et Proclamans.'"

72. Ratzinger, "Constitution on Divine Revelation," 4.

73. "Address to the Pontifical Biblical Commission," April 11, 1991, 3.

74. Harkins, "What Do Syriac/Antiochene Exegesis," 152.

75. Contra DiNoia and Mulcahy, "Scripture and Sacramental Theology," 338, 344. Nevertheless, the divine intent is not limited to that of the human author, as one might conclude from the Flannery translation of *Dei Verbum* 12; the Latin is "*quid hagiographi reapse significare intenderint et eorum verbis manifestare Deo placuerit*" (emphasis added).

76. Healy, "Inspiration and Incarnation."

human nature of Scripture with the two natures of Christ (e.g., Origen, *Commentary on Matthew*, PG 17, 289AB; Maximus the Confessor, *Capita Gnostica* 2.28; *Mystagogia*, 6). The analogy was taken up by Pius XII in *Divino afflante Spiritu* (37), by Vatican Council II in *Dei Verbum* (13), and by Benedict XVI in *Verbum Domini* (19).[77] *Divino afflante Spiritu* (34–35) and *Dei Verbum* (12) have insisted that the point of access to the divine author's intent is that of the human author, or rather of "that which has been expressed directly by the inspired human authors" (*Interpretation of the Bible in the Church* II.B.1.c; cf. I.A.4.g; II.B.1.g; IIIa).[78] John Paul II in his Preface to *Interpretation of the Bible in the Church* said (II.7), "The Church of Christ takes the realism of the incarnation seriously, and this is why she attaches great importance to the 'historical-critical' study of the Bible."[79] "In a theandric reality one can never attain the divine without passing anew by way of the human,"[80] and "no sound theology of inspiration can ever propose a biblical 'monophysitism.'"[81] Hans Urs von Balthasar writes, "The human element represents an immediately available medium for approaching divine revelation."[82] Henri de Lubac maintains, "God acts within history, God reveals himself within history. Even more, God inserts himself within history."[83] In fact, some have named "the historicity of revelation" as one of the most important innovations

[handwritten margin notes: "Only 1 nature b/c JC-dual in incarnate church"; "God and Man relating to / existing by the union of divine + human, — or the joint agency of the divine and human nature."]

77. Healy, "Behind, in Front of," 190–91.

78. Lagrange referred to Augustine on this issue: "*In Scripturis per homines*"; "Les sources," 6–7. To be precise, this "incarnational" nature of Scripture applies to both the "fully human" words *and* the "fully human" history as that history is involved; Semmelroth, "Heilige Schrift als Glaubensquelle," 47.

79. Contra Kerbs, "Método Histórico," 122–23.

80. Cantalamessa, *Mystery of God's Word*, 90; Paglia, *La Bibbia Ridona*, 29, 42, 47; cf. DiNoia and Mulcahy, "Scripture and Sacramental Theology," 342.

81. Farkasfalvy, "Case for Spiritual Exegesis," 342. The terminology is derived from Bouyer, "Où en est le mouvement biblique?"; although the thought is probably more properly called biblical Docetism.

82. Von Balthasar, "Scripture as Word," 13.

83. De Lubac, *Catholicisme*, 119; Rae, *Historiography and Hermeneutics*, 49–63.

of *Dei Verbum*.[84] Avery Dulles writes, "'Historical-critical study' is a tool by which we can most accurately disclose what the sacred writers wanted to say."[85]

Yet Augustine himself admitted we would never really get at authorial intent (*Confessions* 7.25), and it is a mistaken criticism to accuse biblical scholarship of being obsessed with such intent. "That biblical critics have often been intentionalists does not seem to me in doubt,"[86] but intentionalism is only frequent, not inherent. In form criticism of the Psalter, no one cares about the psalms' "original authors"; we have always sought the communities that produced the text.[87] So, too, for traditions history: the interest in traditions of the Pentateuch or Deuteronomistic History is not in authors. We well know that, "The attempt to fix an 'original' meaning is more or less bound to fail."[88] Moreover, "Traditional critics have seldom espoused the view that there is one single meaning in texts that is *the* meaning."[89] Rather, we have restricted meanings to "what they can possibly mean, given the constraints of convention, genre, time . . . There are some things the text cannot mean."[90]

For all its limitations, the historical-critical method remains a necessity.[91] There is nothing to fear here. As. T. K. Cheyne wrote more than a century ago, "No essential truth which He has once revealed can be impaired by any fresh discovery of facts."[92] Christopher Bryan writes:

84. Fisichella, *"Dei Verbum."*

85. Dulles, "Scripture and Magisterium"; cf. Brown, *The Critical Meaning*, 24; Healy, "Behind, in Front of," 187.

86. Barton, *Nature of Biblical Criticism*, 73.

87. Ibid., 7.

88. Ibid., 79.

89. Ibid., 113.

90. Ibid., 113–14.

91. Congregation for the Doctrine of the Faith, *Mysterium Ecclesiae*, 5; Pontifical Biblical Commission, *Interpretation of the Bible in the Church*, 34. The limits and the reasons for its necessity, as delineated in several magisterial documents, are concisely presented in Prior, *Historical Critical Method*, 296.

92. Cheyne, *Hallowing of Criticism*, 205.

No critical question about the Bible, honestly posed, and no critical enquiry, honestly pursued, can be refused by those who claim actually to believe the Bible. Indeed, if we mean what we say about the inspiration of Scripture, we shall expect such questions to lead, sooner or later, to enlightenment.[93]

In fact, almost a century ago, Marie-Joseph Lagrange warned that "the deep cause of Modernism [was] a certain dissatisfaction at the inadequacy of Catholic works that do not tackle certain difficulties."[94] Rigorous scholarly inquiry into the Bible must, in fact, be capable of reaching great truths even without faith, if we hold to the belief that human reason can itself attain a certain truth, as Leo Scheffczyk insisted a quarter-century later.[95]

For this reason, one cannot solve the problem by giving literary criticisms precedence over historical ones. Many have argued that since the historical-critical method means the text is not directed to us and is therefore irrelevant, the only hope for theological applicability is a post-modern synchronic approach.[96] It is true that patristic exegesis and theology did not see history as the primary locus of revelation, and it is true that the so-called School of Antioch prefigured such a non-historical, but non-allegorical, text-centered approach. Nevertheless, the literary approach "does not advance the cause, insofar as literary criticism is engrossed in its own turbid state. The apparent result of . . . [this approach] is a nihilistic relativism."[97] Moreover, "Literature does not exist without a context. Furthermore, literature without a context would lose its content and meaning."[98] If we are interested in the conjunction of the biblical literature and the life of faith, we will necessarily "attempt to posit a context in which the literature functioned as part

93. Bryan, "Preachers and the Critics," 39.

94. Diaries of fall, 1931; cited in Montagne's, *Story of Father Marie-Joseph Lagrange*, 164.

95. Scheffczyk, "Biblische und Dogmatische Theologie."

96. Lategan, "Reader Response Theory," 627.

97. Fretz, *Lamentations and Literary Ethics*, 136.

98. Ibid., 332.

of the [ancient] community's life."[99] Finally, if, as one proponent of such New Literary Criticism has said, it is "easier to go right from the exegesis to the preaching,"[100] there seems little to distinguish this from Fundamentalism.

CONCLUSION

> The pastoral effectiveness of the Church's activity and the spiritual life of the faithful depend to a great extent on the fruitfulness of the relationship between exegesis and theology.   *how defined ?*

So wrote Benedict XVI in *Verbum Domini*, 31. The relationship, however, has had some stormy years, and its fruitfulness is yet to be determined.[101] There is a "need in Biblical interpretation today . . . to recapture an understanding of its role within the Church."[102] I believe "critical biblical scholarship . . . can ground a theology that will express and help to develop the community's self-understanding."[103] The Pontifical Biblical Commission's 1993 *Interpretation of the Bible in the Church* reiterates, "The primary aim of Christian exegesis is to explain the religious message of the Bible, that is, its meaning as the word which God continues to address to the Church and to the entire world (IV.a; III.C.1.b)."[104] The ultimate purpose of Christian exegesis is to nourish and build up the body of Christ with the word of God.[105]   *♀ ♂*

In order to do this, exegesis must be seen as a discipline that exists in a relationship with theology (*Interpretation of the Bible in the Church* III.D.a). It must "provoke theology to deeper insight

99. Ibid.

100. Scullion, "Writings of Francis."

101. The "marital problem" was noticed as early as Blondel, *Letter on Apologetics*, 286.

102. Daley, "Patristic Exegesis," 214.

103. McDonald, "Biblical Scholarship," 127.

104. Williamson, *Catholic Principles*, 148, 343.

105. Williamson, "Catholic Principles for Interpreting Scripture," 2002.

into the divine mystery in response to the work of God's Holy Spirit in the present,"[106] "provid[ing] the other theological disciplines with data fundamental for their operation" (*Interpretation of the Bible in the Church*, III.D.a). Theologians, then, will need to "reformulate, even to reconceptualize, the inceptive biblical" interpretation, as Joseph Fitzmyer writes.[107] *the beginning of something (action)*

In the course of this volume, we shall explore ways in which scholars have attempted to bridge this gap from exegesis to theology using different hermeneutical models. Since each of these models depends on particular understandings of revelation and inspiration, we will first need to discuss briefly the definition of these in the next chapter.

106. Johnson, "Catholic Biblical Scholarship," 7.

107. Fitzmyer, *Scripture*, 81–82.

2

Inspiration

Opuscula - pl., a short work →

INTRODUCTION

There is no reason to include in this book an extensive exposition of the theology of revelation or of the doctrine of inspiration. Many excellent books treat this topic from various perspectives— Catholic,[1] Eastern Orthodox,[2] mainline Protestant,[3] and Evangelical.[4] Such opuscula are best written by historical and systematic theologians, and not by biblical scholars, and the present author is certainly not qualified to complement this collection of works.[5] Nevertheless, in Chapter Three we will see that hermeneutical models build directly on understandings of inspiration and revelation. The precise way in which I propose to examine the hermeneutics of contemporary authors will be particularly dependent on picking out those understandings. It is therefore incumbent to

1. See Paglia, *La Bibbia*; Chapp, *God Who Speaks*; Levering, *Doctrine of Revelation*.

2. Swinburne, *Revelation*.

3. Wolterstorff, *Divine Discourse*.

4. Enns, *Inspiration and Incarnation*; McGowan, *The Bridge*.

5. For an overview of what remains to be done in this area, see Moller, "Biblical Inspiration."

define at least preliminarily and in broad strokes, what is meant by inspiration (and revelation; the two terms will be distinguished shortly).

There are three or perhaps four ways to envision inspiration. We might seek definition or illustrative metaphors by imagining inspiration from God's perspective. This is Active Inspiration, what God is "doing" when he "inspires." Or again, we might look at things from the human perspective, specifically the perspective of the "inspired author" or the text. This is Passive Inspiration, although that term does not imply any sort of "passivity" on the part of the human. Finally, we might view inspiration from the perspective of the biblical text, either a particular passage or the Bible as a whole. This is Terminative Inspiration.[6]

Theoretically, there is another terminus posterior to the text, however: the contemporary reader or listener. That is, we could look at inspiration from the perspective of a modern-day person reading the Bible. This last category is, however, more difficult to work with, most especially since while there is one God, a limited number of texts, and a large but still limited number of human authors, there is no limit to the number and diversity of readers. Moreover, we have already seen in Chapter One some of the dangers of moving our focus too much to the reader. There are a few scholars who have found it helpful to define inspiration from the perspective of the inspired reader,[7] but these are fairly rare. We will therefore focus in this brief chapter on Active, Passive, and Terminative (textual) Inspiration.[8]

6. Hetzenauer, *Wesen und Principien*, 18.

7. Inter alia, Spawn and Wright, *Spirit and Scripture*; Walsh, *Chasing Mystery*; Martin, "Spirit and Flesh"; as well as Martin's essays in *Out of Egypt*, 65–87; and in *Bible and Epistemology*, 43–64. For discussion, see Bovell, "All Scripture."

8. *Dei Verbum* paragraphs 2–6 focus on the latter two, as they treat revelation teleologically; paragraphs 11–13 focus on the former two, looking at inspiration through the lens of agency. Both sections have parallel, Christological conclusions: the incarnation as the *telos* of our own divinization and the incarnation as the analogy for inspiration, as we shall see; Anatolios, "Inspiration and the Fecundity."

THE NATURE OF INSPIRATION

What is quick to frustrate anyone delving into the Catholic definition of inspiration in particular is that the Church has spent far
more time discussing what inspiration is not than what it is. Most
famously, both the models of Subsequent Approval and Divine Assistance have been rejected.

Subsequent Approval, associated largely with Jacques
Bonfrère,[9] holds that "inspiration" is something that happens to
texts after they are written, perhaps at the time of canonization.
There are two different possibilities here. The most commonly
presented view would be that the Church's "approval" of a book,
"subsequent" to its writing, rendering retroactively inspired. In
fact, this view would not require holding that the book was not
inspired at a given year in between its writing and canonization,
since the canonization's "inspiration by subsequent approval"
would inspire the book *at its origin*, in effect telescoping time
and effecting an action at another moment on the continuum of
time. Nevertheless, this view was condemned at the First Vatican
Council. It misunderstands canonization itself: not an ontological
change effected by the Church but recognition by the Church of a
given fact. Just as when saints are canonized they do not by that
act "enter the beatific vision," they are recognized as being in such,
so too when a book is canonized the Church recognizes in that
book the word of God, "has discerned the writings which should
be regarded as sacred Scripture" (*Catechism of the Catholic Church*,
120). The Church has no power to change the nature of a text.

Another kind of Subsequent Approval would be to say that
the Holy Spirit "subsequently approves" an un- (or pre-)inspired
text, rendering it instantly inspired. The Spirit might do this at the
time of canonization, or at some time prior to that but after the
time of the final redactors of the text. Such a view has never been
explicitly condemned, but it is insufficient to account for divine
authorship. It would be difficult to call God the "author" of such
a text.

9. Bonfrère, *Pentateuchis Mosis.*

Divine Assistance, associated with Franz Heinrich Reusch,[10] holds that inspiration simply means that God prevents the human author from falling into error. Yet this cannot be satisfactory. Inspiration is not about inerrancy but about origin. In this case, what would distinguish an infallible Magisterium (leaving aside what that means) from the Bible? This view, too, was condemned at Vatican I.

In terms of positive statements, we must begin simply with inspiration meaning we have God's Word written in human words, destined for human beings (*Dei Verbum* 13; *Verbum Domini* 15.2). Verbal dictation has been repeatedly denied by Catholic tradition going back at least to Origen (*Against Celsus*, 7.3–4) and Epiphanius (*Haer.* 48.1–10). Verbal dictation was only introduced in Catholic circles in the late 1800s, by Thomas Pegues for instance,[11] and widely rejected.

Beyond this, we move into metaphorical language. A document entitled "The Word of God and its Fullness in Christ," issued in November, 1998, by the Vatican Congregation for Clergy, explains the relationship of God's Word to the human words in this way: "This Word, which shows God's condescension and benevolence, in as much as its language has been likened to human language." Here we have a key metaphor for understanding inspiration, "Condescension" (see *Verbum Domini*, 11.2). The idea that inspiration is God's way of lowering himself to a language that might appear unworthy of him, but which he employs because he has in mind not his dignity but our salvation, goes back at least to John Chrysostom, who wrote, "The ordinariness of the words is made necessary by our limitations" (*Homily on Genesis*). So, too, Ephrem the Syrian, who wrote that God works to clothe "himself in our language, so that he might clothe us in his way of life" (*Hymns on Faith* 31.1–2) and spoke of "that Grace which bent down its stature to the level of man's childishness" (*Hymns on Paradise* 11.6–7). Nor is this metaphor uniquely Catholic. John Calvin also spoke of such "accommodation," likening God's inspired word

---

10. Reusch, *Lehrbuch der Einleitung*, 146.
11. Pegues, *Catechism*.

in its biblical form to a parent speaking to their child in baby-talk (*quodammodo balbutire*) (*Sermon* 4 on Job, 63; *Sermon* 63 on Job, 423; *Institutes*, 4.7.5; *Sermon* on John 1:1–5; *Sermon* 18 on 2 Samuel, 155).

Another analogy we have already mentioned in the previous chapter is the Incarnation.[12] This Christological analogy goes back to Maximus the Confessor (*Capita Gnostica*, 2.28; *Mystagogia*, 6): the Word of God became fully human, just as he became a particular individual like us in all things but sin. The analogy appears in *Dei Verbum* 13 and *Verbum Domini* 19. The two realities, divine and human, are maintained intact: Jesus is God and Man indivisible in one Person, so Scripture is indivisibly God's Word in human language.[13] As we have seen earlier, we cannot entertain either a focus on the Scripture as merely a human text (a biblical Arianism), nor one that treats it as merely divine (biblical Docetism).[14]

These two analogies focus on inspiration as a noun, as a condition. But the word "inspiration" derives from a verb, "inspire," which brings us back to Active, Passive, and Terminative Inspiration. Active Inspiration looks at an action of God on the sacred writers. Benedict XV, in *Spiritus Paraclitus* (1920), spoke of this action as cooperation between God and man. We should not misunderstand the word "cooperation," however; it does not mean that part of the work is God's and part man's. There is complete compenetration of action of God and of man. Benedict XV did not intend to provide a theory of inspiration, but he did apply the Instrumental Causality Theory used by Thomas Aquinas in *Summa* 1.1.10.[15] It is another sort of analogy, really, but one that must be used with caution as it is easily misunderstood. When someone uses a tool, there are two causes: the person and the tool—both responsible for the effect. If one writes

---

12. Farkasfalvy, *Inspiration and Interpretation*, 217, 219.

13. Farkasfalvy, "Inspiration and Incarnation."

14. The latter even Paul Claudel succumbed to, when he rejected the view that "the Bible is a human work" *in favor of* "the Bible is a divine work," never considering that it might be both; Claudel, *Essence*, 49–50.

15. Farkasfalvy, *Inspiration and Interpretation*, 214.

on a paper with a pen, both the pen and the writer are responsible
for the mark. The kind of tool used and its quality make a difference in the results produced, and a tool must be used in accordance with what it is. One cannot write on a paper with a mitten
or a cell phone. Now the point of this analogy is not that God is
analogous to the person and the biblical author is analogous to the
pen, a mindless tool that cannot compose anything. We have already dismissed any sort of dictation. The point is that a tool must
be used in accordance with what it is, and a human being is not
a dictation machine or a pen. A human being is a human being.
As Aquinas says in discussing inspiration, "For God provides for
everything according to the capacity of its nature" (*Summa* 1.1.9)
The human writer of Scripture, as the instrumental cause, can
only be inspired by God as a human being, complete with unique
thoughts, free will, imagination, biases, and concerns (what *Dei
Verbum* calls *facultatibus ac viribus suis utentes*), in short, as an
author (*veri auctores*).[16]

Thus, in Inspiration, there are two causes and two authors:
God and the human author (*Verbum Domini*, 19.1).[17] This should
not take us back into the debate about authorial intent, whether
we can find the human author's intent at all, whether that is the
same as the divine author's intent, etc.,[18] because we must recognize that *auctoritas* is as much "authority" as "authorship." When
used by Gregory the Great (*Homilies on Ezekiel* 1, 9), *auctoritas* is a
Roman notion, a personal quality with legal bearing.[19] For Albert
the Great (*Postilla on Isaiah*, prologue), it takes on the nature of a
"cause" (for Albert, primarily the Efficient Cause; for William of
Alton [*Postilla on John*, prologue], the Formal Cause).

16. Farkasfalvy, *Inspiration and Interpretation*, 214. Thus, Cyril of Alexandria (*In John*, 1.10, 18) refers to John's efforts to adapt his writings to the goals
he had formulated for his Gospel (also Augustine, *Sermons*, 246.1).

17. *Dei Verbum* stated *Deus auctor scripturae* but reserved the term "*vere
auctoris*" for the human author, while *Verbum Domini* uses this term for God
as well; Farkasfalvy, "How to Complete."

18. Farkasfalvy, *Inspiration and Interpretation*, 220–21.

19. Bellamah, "Late Medieval Perspectives."

Turning to Passive Inspiration (*Ex parte hominis*), we will need to distinguish between prophetic inspiration and biblical inspiration. The inspiration of the prophet, because he knows he is commissioned by God to preach and communicate to others what *prophet* he receives, necessarily implies revelation (*revelatio activa*).[20] The biblical writer does not necessarily know himself to be the instrument of God (2 Macc 2:24; Luke 1:1–4), since as we have seen, he acts as God's instrument but in accord with his own nature, neither constrained nor compelled.

Both prophetic inspiration and biblical inspiration have their object in revelation (*ad docendum / ad loquendum*), but biblical inspiration always has its end in the writing of a text (*ad scribendum*).[21] According to everything we have learned about oral tradition from biblical scholarship, especially of the Old Testament, that writing is surely a late development in the history of revelation.[22] These points become clear when we compare, for example, Elijah with Jeremiah, bracketing issues of historicity for the time being. Elijah had only prophetic inspiration; Jeremiah had prophetic inspiration to preach and to at least some degree biblical inspiration in writing.

We must now, however, distinguish inspiration from revelation. They are two different things. Thus, "Jesus Christ is the apex of God's revelation, but he did not write anything."[23] On the other hand, inspiration does not have for its object the giving of any new knowledge to the writer; rather, its object is to enable him to write down by God's authority what he already knows, either naturally (e.g., Acts 9) or through revelation (whether indirect or direct).

One aspect of Passive Inspiration is the effect of the action of God on the intellect of the sacred writer. The author uses the same intellectual processes under inspiration as a profane writer would. God elevates these faculties to himself, in different manner

20. This is much discussed by later Scotists, e.g., Krisper, *Theologia Scholae Scotisticae*, 88 = tractate 4, quaestio 1, no. 10.

21. W. Harrington, "Word of God."

22. Miller, *Oral Tradition*, 43–47.

23. Gresch, "Further Reflections," 82.

for different authors.[24] Thus, inspiration takes place differently in different texts,[25] as Augustine understood, holding that one could not answer *how* a text was true until after studying that text.[26] "Every literary genre has its own way of being true."[27]

Finally, we turn to Terminative Inspiration (*Ex parte termini*), special divine assistance in the book's composition. The advantage of this perspective is that inspiration is extended to everything that contributes to the written expression of thought, all the tradents and glossers and redactors, including all who contribute to the work at a later date.[28] We affirm that God wrote through the many different people over a long time who edited the story, changed the emphasis, added details, and reflected on its meaning. God inspired all of them, not just the earliest authors (e.g., the unglossed *Urtexte*) or the final form. And yet there are "high points of actual inspiration over and above the Spirit's providential guidance during the formative process,"[29] and the final form is one of these.

THE EXTENT OF INSPIRATION

This matter merits some brief discussion without venturing too far into the issue of inerrancy. The nineteenth-century "Jesuit School" of Johann Baptist Franzelin[30] distinguished between the *res* (contents) and *form* of Scripture, and denied inspiration to at least some of the form. This seems to be a denial of the findings of psychology. Although the idea and the word used to express it are distinct, they are not separable. They generally constitute in our consciousness an undivided whole.

24. Lagrange, "Une Pensée"; Bea, "Inspiration et Révélation," 504–5.

25. Gresch, "Further Reflections," 83.

26. Murphy, "*Dei Verbum*."

27. Gresch, "Further Reflections," 87.

28. Ibid., 82–83.

29. Ibid., 84.

30. Franzelin, *De Divina Traditione*.

Another limiting of the extent of inspiration, proposed even by John Henry Newman,[31] was to distinguish between texts about faith and morals and passages about other things. Leo XIII's 1893 *Providentissimus Deus* was a reaction especially to an article by the rector of the Institut Catholique of Paris, d'Hulst, summing up those positions.[32] Leo wrote, "It would be utterly impious to limit inspiration to some portions only of Sacred Scripture . . . Nor can one tolerate the method of those who extricate themselves from difficulties by allowing without hesitation that divine inspiration extends to matters of faith and morals and to nothing more" (II.D.3). Benedict XV's 1920 *Spiritus Paraclitus* likewise condemned those who "believe that only what deals with religion is intended and taught by God in the Scriptures."

Whatever *Dei Verbum* 11 means when it says, "The books of Scripture must be acknowledged as teaching firmly, faithfully, and without error that truth which God wanted put into the sacred writings for the sake of our salvation,"[33] it does not intend to restrict inspiration to specific texts.[34]

But here our discussion, were it to continue, would move into the subject of inerrancy, which is not germane to the chapters that

31. Newman, "Inspiration of Scripture," 185–99.

32. D'Hulst, "La Question biblique."

33. *Cum ergo omne id, quod auctores inspirati seu hagiographi asserunt, retineri debeat assertum a Spiritu Sancto, inde Scripturae libri veritatem, quam Deus nostrae salutis causa Litteris Sacris consignari voluit, firmiter, fideliter et sine errore docere profitendi sunt.*

34. The most straightforward reading is that it limits the inerrancy of *all* passages qualitatively. It does not limit inerrancy quantitatively to certain passages, but it also is not merely a teleological statement. This is suggested by the official footnotes to Thomas Aquinas, *On Truth* Q.12, A.2, C, and Augustine, *Literal Interpretation of Genesis* 2, 9, 20. It is certainly the way the sentence has been understood by John Paul II (see his October 3, 1981, Address to the Pontifical Academy of Sciences) and Benedict XVI (see Wicks, "Six texts," 280; Ratzinger, *God and the World*, 153; Benedict XVI, "Message." May 2, 2011; Easter Vigil Homily, April 23, 2011). For discussion of this reading, see Farkasfalvy, *Inspiration and Interpretation*, 227–28, 232. For a contrary reading that sees no limitation of inerrancy here, see Hahn, "Sake of Our Salvation," 33–34; Harrison, "Restricted Inerrancy," 233, 240; and Pitre, "Mystery of God's Word," 56–60.

follow. We shall begin these with a move from definitions of inspiration to hermeneutical models.

3

Hermeneutical Models

INTRODUCTION

It is imperative that "the results of critical historical inquiries into the text of the Bible . . . be appropriated by theological exegesis";[1] and that is what the Church has asked us to do (*Dei Verbum*, no. 12; *Interpretation of the Bible in the Church* III.B.2.b, h, k; III.C.1.b; IV.a). Francis Martin notes the great potential for historical-critical methods to "facilitate the communicative effort of the text itself."[2] Twenty years ago, Raymond Brown neatly delineated the difference between exegesis and hermeneutics as the distinction between what the text once "meant" and what it "means" to-day.[3] However, this is not as accurate as seeing it as a "gap" "between what was once achieved, intended, or "shown," and what might be achieved, intended, or "shown" today."[4] We ought not to describe the theological appropriation of higher criticism of the Bible as a

1. DiNoia and Mulcahy, "Scripture and Sacramental Theology," 330. Cf. McDonald, "Biblical Scholarship," 126; Farkasfalvy, "Case for Spiritual Exegesis," 349.

2. Martin, "Literary Theory," 593.

3. Brown, *Critical Meaning*, 23–44.

4. Fowl and Jones, *Reading in Communion*, 61; Kelsey, "Theological Use."

distinction between what the text "meant" and now "means." "We are not searching for what the [texts] . . . meant but have now ceased to mean; we are searching for what they actually mean, as opposed to what . . . they might be thought to mean,"[5] "not constrained by prior convictions about the text's meaning . . . (which *includes* the scholarly guild)."[6] While the historical-critical method adroitly bridges the historical gap between our world and the world of the Bible by historical analogy, in a way literary criticisms do not, it is not sufficient to bridge the theological gap.[7]

There have, in fact, been many attempts to bridge the impasse, to use the metaphor I began with. Some, like Christine Helmer, see a gap requiring "a bridge,"[8] or even an "iron curtain," as Brevard Childs says;[9] for others it is a mere "boundary" to be crossed.[10] Benedict XVI called it a "sometimes a barrier" in *Verbum Domini* 35.Yet it would not be safe to go from historical criticism to theology "without invoking an intermediary scheme to establish the connection."[11] I prefer the metaphor of a road. The title of this book comes from a rejected title for a chapter in *Lord of the Rings* that recounted how various parties came from the defeat of Saruman to the siege of Gondor. The "roads" tried in the past can be grouped into categories. Admittedly, this immediately introduces generalization and reduction. The categories used here derive from looking at hermeneutics using a communication analogy.

5. Barton, *Nature*, 83.

6. Ibid., 124.

7. Fretz, *Lamentations,* 327, 328. Analogies in the theological realm nevertheless "require familiarity with both the ancient and the modern context" (Fretz, *Lamentations,* 338). Kelsey denies there is any gap, since a) "There is constant material change through the history of doctrine"; and b) "It suppresses the freedom of the Spirit to bring new truth out of the texts"; Kelsey, "Theological Use."

8. Helmer, "Biblical Theology," 175 and passim; Matthews, "When We Remembered Zion," 93.

9. Childs, *Biblical Theology in Crisis,* 141–42.

10. Ibid., 300.

11. Helmer, "'Open Systems.'"

COMMUNICATION MODELS FOR REVELATION

Defining inspiration as God's word in human words and refer-
ring to Scripture as the "Word" of God implies a communication
between God and human beings. Revelation, therefore, is communication, and this more broadly than written communication:
as Farkasfalvy writes, "The primary paradigm of the mystery that
a theology of inspiration must treat is not that of the 'God Who
Writes' but of the 'God Who Speaks.'"[12] Let me begin with an old
but useful model for language, then.

In 1918, Karl Bühler schematized language as a triad of
functions, corresponding to three poles of the communication,
Darstellung, Auslösung, and *Kundgabe*.[13] *Darstellung* or "repre-
sentation" refers to the expressed content of communication, that
which can be objectively described by an observer.[14] *Auslösung*,
or "inciting signal," is that element of communication that provokes a response in the hearer.[15] *Kundgabe*, "notification," is an
element in the hearers themselves, a manifestation of the person's
interior attitude.[16] René Latourelle, in 1966, applied Bühler's triad
to divine-human communication, identifying different aspects of
revelation as Word (*Darstellung*), Testimony (*Auslösung*), and Encounter (*Kundgabe*).[17]

Without reference to Bühler, Avery Dulles outlined five elements of communication and then divided hermeneutical methodologies according to which of the five elements is most emphasized
when looking at the divine-human communication.[18] Christine
Helmer produced a similar schema, without reference to Dulles or
Bühler, and her element list is similar to Dulles's.[19] Both of their

12. Farkasfalvy, *Inspiration and Interpretation*, 204.

13. Bühler, *Die geistige Entwicklung*.

14. Ibid., 52–56.

15. Ibid., 4, 60, 94.

16. Ibid., 293–95, 307–9.

17. Latourelle, *Theology of Revelation*, 315–27.

18. Dulles, *Models of Revelation*, chaps. 1–2.

19. Helmer, "Biblical Theology."

lists of elements can be constructively linked to Bühler's triad. For convenience, I use Dulles's terminology so that each element is labelled, in English, with a word beginning with "E."

First, there is an "Encounter." There is a historical fact of a meeting between parties. Second, this Encounter is an "Event"; it has a relevance to the parties in this Encounter.[20] If we were to ask someone whom they had seen on a given day, they will not list every person who entered their field of vision, but only those meetings that had an impact. But it is not Event but "Experience" that corresponds to *Kundgabe*. The reason an Encounter is an Event is that it provokes an Experience within the receiver of the communication. Notice the distinction. The Event exists observable to all, although not everyone may know if a given Encounter is an Event. The Experience is observable only to one of the two parties of the communication. Many communications will have an "Expression."[21] This is the *Darstellung*, the record or fixation of the "subjective construal of the reality that has made an impact."[22] Finally, there is an "Expectation" of the Encounter recurring; this is the *Auslösung*.[23]

For revelation, human-divine communication, there is an "Encounter," a historical revelation or revelatory act that functions as a meeting between God and humanity. To compare this with terms used in Chapter Two, this refers to Active Inspiration. This Encounter is an "Event"; there is relevance to at least some human beings for this Encounter (thus excluding so-called "General Revelation" or "Natural Theology" here).[24] We are here dealing with Passive Inspiration. Again, the reason an Encounter is an Event for those specific human beings is that it provokes an Experience within the receiver. Now those receivers include not only those first-generation witnesses to the divine communication, but later hearers and eventually readers for whom this "revelation" is nev-

20. Dulles, *Models of Revelation*, 195–96.
21. Ibid., 193–95.
22. Helmer, "Biblical Theology," 177.
23. Dulles, *Models of Revelation*, 199–201.
24. Helmer, "Biblical Theology," 177; Dulles, *Models of Revelation*, chap. 4.

ertheless a new Event. They undergo their own Experience. Thus, this allows us to include an element we were forced to omit from the Active/Passive/Terminative triad, i.e., the locus of revelation being a divine action on a later reader of the biblical text. The parallels with human communication hold true with the elements of Encounter, Event, and Experience: the Event exists observable to all, although not everyone may know if a given Encounter is an Event. The Experience is observable only to the human we are considering, be it sacred writer or prophet—which is naturally beyond our reach—or believing reader. The reason we are interested in the Bible is that this divine-human communication has an Expression,[25] a *Darstellung*, a textual fixation that is also "an anthropological necessity."[26] Finally, because God has continued to reveal over time, and God's communication with humanity did not cease with the death of the last New Testament writer, there is an "Expectation" of the Encounter recurring; this is the *Auslösung*.[27]

Dulles then divides hermeneutical methodologies according to which of the five elements is most emphasized, placing biblical theologians in each of the five "E's." He also has a sixth category into which he places himself and to which we shall return. This book will not use all six categories, for several reasons. First, Dulles's "Revelation as Encounter" category only loosely describes the scholars he places into it. Dulles uses this category to designate the dialectic theologians in the tradition of Karl Barth and Emil Brunner. I would argue that Encounter *is* an Experience-Event, that any Encounter we have with God is by nature the "gaze of the other" as Ricoeur says,[28] and what makes the dialectic theologians distinct is merely their way of describing the Experience-driven Eventness of the Encounter. This may not be entirely clear, but it is even less clear how the dialectic theologians correspond to "Encounter" as Dulles initially describes it in the communications analogy.

---

25. Dulles, *Models of Revelation*, chap. 3.

26. Helmer, "Biblical Theology," 177.

27. Dulles, *Models of Revelation*, 27–30, and chap. 7; Helmer, "Biblical Theology," 176.

28. See discussion of Ricoeur in McLean, *Biblical Interpretation*, 309.

Second, while Dulles can find scholars to place in the Revelation as Encounter and Revelation as Experience categories, neither of these "roads" has been popular among biblical theologians in the last half-century. Rather than meriting their own chapters, therefore, these—and Dulles's sixth model, one without an "E," a symbolic hermeneutic he proposed in several other venues,[29] can be dealt with briefly at this point.

Dulles' "symbolic" approach begins with the same model of revelation as the Encounter model.[30] The text, as with any communication, is both intelligible and not intelligible, and it is mediated by symbols. The emphasis is on symbolic mediation, and in both the content of the revelation is Christ as Word of the Father.[31]

What Dulles calls the Encounter model, going back to Karl Barth, views the symbolic mediation in a dialectic way because of God's dual transcendence and immanence.[32] God is both concealed and revealed by the text, the compositional history of which is far too long for us to worry about authors: the process is inspired.[33] The Bible is the Word in that Jesus the Word speaks through it, so the text is the Word of God only as it is preached and received through grace, as it draws the reader into the dialectic of its own search after truth, challenging him the further it proceeds, stimulating his appetite enough to entice him into dialogue, thus ensuring that the revelation will continue.[34] Therefore, it is not the Word when "the seed falls along the path"; Barth writes, "The Bible is the witness of divine revelation . . . We distinguish the Bible as such from revelation."[35]

29. Dulles, "Symbol"; Dulles, *Revelation Theology*, 138–46.

30. Dulles, *Models of Revelation*, chap. 9 and 201–5.

31. Ibid., 86, 88.

32. Barth, *Church Dogmatics*, I/2, 458; Dulles, *Models of Revelation,* chap. 6 and 197–99.

33. Dulles, *Models of Revelation,* 198.

34. Barth, *Church Dogmatics*, I/2, 457, 463; Dulles, *Models of Revelation*, 87–88, 92, 198.

35. Barth, *Church Dogmatics*, I/2, 462–63.

Hans Conzelmann picked up the dialectic hermeneutic from Barth, as did Georg Strecker.[36] Among Catholics, it was developed by Luis Alonso Schökel. He explained that revelation was "mediated by the language" in a "dialogical process."[37] The symbolic mediation is an "obscure light of mystery . . . remain[ing] open to the inquiry and ever deeper penetration of the faithful."[38] "Information is accidental."[39] More recently, this dialectic approach— a dialogue with the symbolic text—has been applied by biblical scholar Francisco Garcia-Treto and moralist Servais Pinckaers.[40]

Some modern exegetes espouse this model. Luke Timothy Johnson emphasizes the "symbols of the Scripture."[41] Sandra Schneiders has extensively developed this hermeneutic.[42] She explains that the biblical symbol "participates directly in the presence and power of that which it symbolizes."[43] In this, we have C. S. Lewis' theory of "transposition," in which the symbol "can actually be drawn into the higher [symbolized] and become part of it."[44] John Donahue's view of parables as metaphorical discourse interpreted by literary context seems similar.[45] *stating an inference*

Dulles himself views symbolic mediation not in a dialectic way but an "illative" one. The biblical symbols are still both intelligible and not intelligible, but because revelation is a multivalent, *many interpretations* partially knowable token/representation. The symbolic-but-not-dialectic model is that which Dulles himself chose.[46] Dulles traces this model to Romano Guardini's theology of revelation mediated

36. Conzelmann, *Theology of the New Testament*, xiii, 7; Strecker, *Theology of the New Testament*, 8.

37. Alonso Schökel, *Manual of Hermeneutics*, 53, 69, 77.

38. Alonso Schökel, *Inspired Word*, 322.

39. Ibid., 315.

40. Garcia-Treto, "Crossing the Line," 105–16; Pinckaers, *Morality*, 8.

41. Johnson, *Living Gospel*, 8; Johnson, *Real Jesus*, 174.

42. Schneiders, *Revelatory Text*, 45, 113.

43. Ibid., 35–36.

44. Lewis, *Weight of Glory*, 27.

45. Donahue, *Gospel in Parable*, 1, 25–26.

46. Dulles, "Symbol," 1.

through symbols and to Reginald Garrigou-Lagrange's distinction between revelation and the subjective act of its reception.[47] Dulles' symbol "points to a reality behind itself. But this other reality is one which cannot be precisely described or defined; it is not knowable . . . except in and through the symbol."[48] We read the symbols with various tools: critical scholarship, Tradition, and Christian experience.[49] Karl Rahner developed a similar theory of revelation, promoted later by Monika Hellwig.[50]

Both varieties of this model solve the problem that revelation came about not only by acts and words but also by images.[51] Both allow historicity to be of lesser importance.[52] They require the interpreter be a believer: "the lower medium can be understood only if we know the higher medium."[53] They allow the text to work simultaneously on the intellect, "the imagination, the will, and the emotions."[54] Although they allow the text's symbols to transcend time and place, they also serve as a basis for changing "symbols shaped by the constant rereading of the scripture"[55] in order to re-contextualize the biblical message for today, since "the overwhelming realities of revelation are such that they can never be contained within a single set of terms."[56] The models have proven useful for theologians like Hellwig and moralists like Richard Gula.

On the other hand, what, exactly is a symbol? Is it merely a "never adequate"[57] simile or an efficacious sacrament? Is it true that "it is more correct to say that the Bible is potentially revelatory

47. Dulles, *Revelation Theology*, 146, 138.

48. Dulles, "Symbol," 2, 5.

49. Verdes, "Ética Bíblica y Hermenéutica," 330–34.

50. Rahner, "Concept of Revelation," 21; Hellwig, "Bible Interpretation," 179.

51. Dulles, "Symbol," 5; cf. *Catechism of the Catholic Church*, 117.

52. Dulles, "Symbol," 6.

53. Lewis, *The Weight of Glory*, 22.

54. Dulles, "Symbol," 3; Johnson, *Real Jesus*, 174.

55. Johnson, *Living Gospel*, 8.

56. Dulles, "Symbol," 24–25.

57. Hellwig, "Bible Interpretation," 187; Donahue, *Gospel in Parable*, 25.

than to say that it is revelation?"[58] This model avoids the issue of just *how* God is revealed. Is the text symbolic, or are the events it recounts, or both?[59] Do we ever access that which is symbolized? If not, what is our faith grounded in?[60] The model leaves open the response expected of us to the symbol. *Who* is doing the actualizing? If reason matters in this process, the model will yield an elite of symbol-readers, capable of finding "the hermeneutical key which unlocks the true meaning of the text."[61]

We can also briefly deal with Revelation as Experience. Francis Martin has explored hermeneutical models focusing on the *Kundgabe* or inner experience, as noted earlier, as have occasional others.[62] Martin calls this "critical hermeneutics of the Spirit."[63] As Kern Robert Trembath states,

> If inspiration itself is the name of an experience of being divinely spirated—i.e., realizing in one's own personal history that one really is the self whom God's Self intended—then inspired texts are the literary agents through which those who experience the self-Self relationship now can be historically assured of sharing that experience with their ancestors who recorded their experiences for precisely this sense of assurance.[64]

The content of revelation is an experience of God, not a set of details. Affections are vital to this hermeneutic, which is controlled by the belief that God is speaking to us through his Word and by his Spirit.[65] Revelation occurs in the context of devotion to God and a desire for obedience and faithfulness, while Scripture is transforming, efficacious, powerful, life-changing, and "can en-

---

58. Schneiders, *Revelatory Text*, 39.

59. Dulles, "Symbol," 3, 6.

60. Dulles, *Models of Revelation*, 94, 96–97.

61. Gula, *Reason Informed*, 168. Dulles, *Models of Revelation*, 95. An example is Güttgemanns's, *Candid Questions*, 271, 287–92.

62. See above, p. 20 n. 7.

63. Martin, "Spirit and Flesh," 6, 26, 30.

64. Trembath, "Gabel's 'Inspiration and Truth,'" 87.

65. Martin, "Spirit and Flesh," 6.

gender a distinct set of affections."[66] We do not critique the text; the
text critiques us, judges us.[67] Tillich, paradigmatic of the theology
behind this model, wrote, "Revelation becomes more revealing the
more it speaks . . . to the special receptivity of his [the Christian's]
mind."[68] Conversely, Martin states, "the flesh interferes with our
understanding of what the Scriptures are telling us."[69] Martin presents the role of higher criticism in the hermeneutic as testing and
verifying "a truly divinely conferred insight."[70] It would appear that
Roland Murphy also eventually went this route, when he spoke in
2001 of actualizing "a 'spiritual' application: the potential of the
text to affect our relationship with God."[71]

Although there is much in common between this and the
Expression model, this model's distinctiveness is that "the expe-
riential referent of that text in direct relationship to the sense of
the text now seems the proper route for analyzing the revelatory
experiences disclosed by the first-order revelation-languages in
the Scriptures," according to David Tracy.[72]

In favor of this model, much of Scripture is poetry, minister-
ing at the emotive level. This model gives interpretation a claim on
people—it is what most care about. It yields (and requires) piety,
love, prayer.[73] Charles Curran and William Spohn have found it
useful for moral theology.[74] It is consistent with Scripture: "For the
word of God is quick and powerful . . ." (Hebrews 4:12), "Did not
our heart burn within us, while he talked with us by the way, and
while he opened to us the scriptures?" (Luke 24:32; cf. Psalm 95:7;
Hebrews 12:25) and with Tradition. Aquinas wrote, "Those who

66. Spohn, *Scripture and Ethics*, 110; cf. Martin, "Spirit and Flesh," 10.

67. Spohn, *Scripture and Ethics*, 90.

68. Tillich, *Biblical Religion*, 3.

69. Martin, "Spirit and Flesh," 12.

70. Ibid., 12.

71. Murphy, *Biblical Heritage*, 5; cf. 6.

72. Tracy, *On Naming the Present*, 111.

73. Martin, "Spirit and Flesh," 13.

74. Curran, *Fundamental Moral Theology*, 9, 24; "Role and Function,"
180, 186; Spohn, *Scripture and Ethics*, 91.

could interpret what was written down . . . [their work] must be done by divine grace, just as the original revelation took place by the grace of God" (*Summa contra Gentiles*, 3.154). *Dei Verbum* 8 and 12 say that the soul of Tradition is to be found in the action of the Holy Spirit by which those divine realities handed on are rendered present.

But this model appears to be a method with no kerygmatic content and no integrated hermeneutical system. Furthermore, it sets up a Hinduistic hierarchy of states of the initiate. It could lead to personal infallibility;[75] if, "The role of the Bible is to be seen in the light of cognitive and noncognative affective experiences of the reader,"[76] the risk of subjectivity is enormous, and there is little basis to reject even Gerhard Kittel's anti-Semitic 1933 *Das Antike Weltjudentum*. Finally, is it consistent with the aim of revelation in the first place? Trembath says, "Scripture's normativity resides in measuring or testing the relationship between persons and God."[77] G. Ernest Wright writes, "Was their aim that of obtaining a knowledge of God, or were they for the purpose of securing a knowledge of one's vocation? . . . What of the great experience of Isaiah? Was it solely the prophet's feeling of God's holiness and his own sin? . . . Knowledge and truth in the Bible involve things to do, not simply . . . an experience of the God within."[78] It is also worthwhile to note that, "the concept of the *Spirit of God* as a medium of revelation is less stressed in the Bible."[79]

So Encounter, Experience, and Symbol are omitted from the chapters that follow. At the same time, I have added two other categories that Dulles does not treat. The first is a variety of Expression, and that is what is inaccurately called Canonical Criticism. It fits into the communication analogy under the rubric of Expression in the following way. What Dulles (and I) designate by the Revelation as Expression hermeneutic is a focus on the text itself

75. Wright and Fuller, *Acts of God*, 21.

76. McKnight, "Reader–Response Criticism," 205–6.

77. Trembath, "Gabel's 'Inspiration and Truth,'" 88.

78. Wright and Fuller, *Acts of God*, 21–22.

79. Mowinckel, *Old Testament as Word*, 44.

as the locus of revelation, the actual words on the biblical page. Revelation as Canon merely moves that text focus to the entire biblical canon. Thus, the locus of revelation is still an Expression, but it is no longer a given biblical passage or even a single book. Only the entire canon as a whole equals revelation, or serves as the locus of revelation.

The other category added here is Revelation in Ecclesia—the name chosen to preserve the "E's." This is a sort of Revelation as Experience, except that the locus of revelation is not an individual believing hearer but the faith community. Revelation occurs not when a person reads (or when a prophet is inspired or a text written), but when the Church reads, when a person reads in community. As we shall see, this is now an important hermeneutical model in the field.

Some further points ought to be made about the communication analogy that are not clear in Dulles. There is an entire history of Encounters, which are personal for new people in each generation because of their own Event/Experience resonance. This history of Encounters is not a dialogue, God-humanity, but a trialogue with the Bible (Expression) also included. The conversation is now God and humanity and Bible. So Revelation is both process and product, and this Expression is in itself another Encounter.

Despite its weaknesses, this analogy rubric does highlight some key questions that biblical theology must address. Is the Bible the record of God's revelatory acts, or is the Bible the revelation? Did God speak to Israel by giving the Ten Commandments or by inspiring writers to write the history of giving the Ten Commandments? Or does God speak to us via the Holy Spirit when we read that text? When we read it alone or in/with the Church?

In the chapters that follow, five models will be examined, in the following order. Revelation as Expression will come first, since the biblical text is what we have before us; everything else must be reconstructed. Revelation as Canon will be treated second, as a subcategory of Expression. Then discussion will move to Revelation as Event, in this case the historical events of ancient Israel.

Revelation as Expectation and then Revelation in Ecclesia will follow that.

Some evaluation will be made of each of these models. This evaluation will be terms of the concordance between the model and the definition of inspiration given in this chapter, the insistence upon the historical-critical method elucidated in Chapter One, and the potential for the given hermeneutic to produce something of use to theologians. I am mindful of what Rex Mason said of H. Wheeler Robinson: "We have to pay those who have preceded us the courtesy of not lashing them with critical whips which later knowledge and subsequent movements of thought have put into our hands."[80] Moreover, I "recognize the plurality of interpretive practices without granting epistemological primacy to any of them."[81] A sixth model, a new model proposed here building on the work of diverse scholars, will draw on all of the preceding five.

In my survey of these roads, I do not discuss every biblical theologian.[82] Greater attention is given to Catholic exegetes, as *Catholic* Catholic biblical theology is the focus of this book. The book is also focused on the Old Testament. This is not solely because I am *OT* an Old Testament scholar and wary of labelling scholars who are not my peers. It is also because New Testament theology, for better or worse, has not experienced the difficulties that Old Testament *true?* theology has. I would suggest this is for the worse. As Moore and Sherwood have noted, "For the overwhelming majority of New Testament scholars it has sufficed to gloss, paraphrase, amplify,

---

80. Mason, "Robinson Revisited," 220.

81. Tucker, "Biblical Exegesis."

82. I deliberately exclude those who must be labeled eisegetes. Although others have given this label to theologians like Bouyer and von Balthasar (Fitzmyer, *Scripture*, 91), I do not. But I will give it to those who add to the text, be it one who writes into Genesis 3 "a life–threatening serpent, with his evil stealth, to deliver what Adam rightly took to be a thinly veiled threat to his life" (Hahn, *Father Who Keeps*, 69), or one who rewrites every occurrence of "man" in 1 Corinthians 11:2–16 as "human being" in order to make it less sexist (Murphy–O'Connor, "Sex and Logic," 482–500; "Interpolation," 81–94; "Once Again," 265–74).

annotate, or otherwise elaborate on the theology, Christology, pneumatology, ecclesiology, and eschatology of the New Testament authors."[83]

Finally, let me admit that forcing a host of biblical theologians into five or six categories is oversimplifying and reductionist. I have been criticized for doing so in oral presentations that developed into this book. Yet such schematization is the only way to distill a large body of theoretical work, and it allows us to examine the nuances that divide these approaches, showing ultimately that they are not necessarily antithetical.[84]

mutually incompatible

83. Moore and Sherwood, "Biblical Studies," 105.

84. Linkon, "Reader's Apprentice."

4

Revelation as Expression

The first model is to view Revelation primarily as Expression.[1] The text and its set of truths are the revelation, or as Dulles clarifies, revelation is complete when it is communicated definitively in the original manuscripts of the biblical text, and perhaps when it is preserved.[2] To some, the text's historicity is important, to others, like Horst Dietrich Preuss, it is more important what the Bible says than what its characters may or may not have ever done.[3] We will have to ask shortly whether it is possible to have a poetic witness like this without a referential witness.

An early example of this is Walter Eichrodt's theology of the Old Testament. His method was synthetic: a "complete picture of the OT realm of belief . . . completed in Christ."[4] This search for a "unifying principle"[5] and "structural unity"[6] became, for Gerhard

---

1. Dulles, *Models of Revelation*, chap. 3 and 193–95.

2. Ibid., 42, 45.

3. Preuss, *Old Testament Theology*; Gorospe, *Narrative and Identity*; Bell, "Re–constructing Babel," 519–68.

4. Eichrodt, *Theology of the Old Testament*, 25–27.

5. Ibid., 28.

6. Ibid., 31.

von Rad, a diverse theology of the Bible. Rather than "the" theological outlook of the OT, this was an account of Israel's faith that
was not static, either chronologically or by genre.[7] Later scholars
like Lawrence Boadt and now Paul House stress one theme (*Mitte
der Schrift*) or a few main themes instead of surveying all of them.[8]

It would be a mistake to think that such approaches are long
past. The idea that the text itself is the revelation, "freed from an
obsession with historical fact,"[9] and that we can get theology
directly from its expression is common in various incarnations.
Thus Diane Bergant says the Scriptures "reveal characteristics of
God," whom "we see" in the text.[10] Daniel Harrington is looking
for Eichrodt's "unifying concept," the "overarching theme for the
Bible."[11] Some of the neo-expressionist interpretations are based
on postmodern synchronic approaches that are tightly tied to the
text and its structural analysis.[12] For such, "theological reading is
part of the text's semantic, grammatical and linguistic features."[13]
The important point is that the narrative produces the meaning,
not the author.[14]

There are several advantages to this method. It is consistent,
turning away from imposing theological categories directly from

7. Von Rad, *God at Work*, 14–15. It would be mistaken to see von Rad as a
pioneer of the *Heilsgeschichte* approach to which we will return. His quest for
"testimonies" of faith stated, "even less can the history of this world of faith
be the subject of the theology of the Old Testament" (*Old Testament Theology*, 111), a view those partial to the "salvation history" road would not share.
Israel's history did not, for von Rad, "present any kind of meaningful pattern";
Old Testament Theology, 418.

8. Boadt, *Reading the Old Testament*, 543–52; House, "God's Design," 32.

9. Helmer, "Biblical Theology," 183.

10. Bergant, *People of the Covenant*, 171–72. In her commentaries, Bergant
sees Qohelet talking directly to us; *Job, Ecclesiastes*, 292.

11. D. J. Harrington, *Interpreting the Old Testament*, 135, 137; cf. also
Caird, *New Testament Theology*.

12. Scullion, "Writings of Francis." Other examples include P. D. Miller,
Way of the Lord, 306.

13. Helmer, "Biblical Theology," 182.

14. Wénin, "Analyse Narrative," 45–57.

dogmatic theology.[15] It has a basis in Scripture and Tradition.[16] Gregory of Nyssa's *akolouthia* or "sequence/structure" of a text was central to his hermeneutic (*Hexameron*, 44.68, 71, 81a). Gregory's *theōria* are to be found within the literal verbal narrative details. The text is not a vehicle that refers to something outside its verbal structure—be it spiritual patterns (as it was for Origen and Augustine) or profane history (as for us) *or even author's intent*—but the text is to be elucidated by following verbal clues and webs of exposition (*Homily 1 on Ecclesiastes*, J283.5–17; 301.3—303.2).[17] Thus, it opens interpretation up to multiple senses but with the control that they are all senses *in* the text.[18]

It also provides the basis for a method to do theology and is fruitful for mission and growth,[19] and has been particularly attractive to moral theologians like Germain Grisez who hold that "a precise set of words controls" meaning,[20] "to identify the propositions in the Bible that could be used as premises."[21] The text's own fixity enables theologians to go beyond preconceived notions of what the Bible says.[22]

However, there are many problems. Though one could see the hermeneutical task as one of faith,[23] the method can exist without faith,[24] as a mere survey of the religion of past peoples.[25] Heikki Räisänen used it consciously without "critical sympathy"

15. Rendtorff, "Von Rad's Contribution," 351.

16. Dulles, *Models of Revelation,* 46. It is, in fact, explicitly the model of the rejected draft *De Fontibus Revelationis* that became Vatican II's *Dei Verbum: Acta Synodalia Sacrosancti Concilii Oecumenici Vaticani II*, vol. 1.3 (Congregatio Generalis 19; Rome: Typis Polyglottis Vaticanis, 1971), 17.

17. These are not Origen's *gnoses*, even if some of Gregory's allegories are unwieldily complex.

18. Osiek, "Catholic or catholic?," 21.

19. Dulles, *Models of Revelation*, 47.

20. Grisez, *Beyond the New Theism,* 364.

21. Grisez and Boyle, "Responses to Our Critics," 233.

22. Bell, "Reconstructing Babel," 547–49.

23. Von Rad, *Biblical Interpretations in Preaching*, 12.

24. De Vaux, "Is It Possible?" 56.

25. Lohfink, "Alttestamentliche Wissenschaft als Theologie?," 15.

or "genuine interest."[26] When faith is brought in, it becomes the homiletic "interpretation" we discussed in Chapter One.[27] We are back to "recover from scripture 'valuable theological insights' that may have relevance for today,"[28] or, conversely, "how our lives . . . might fitly answer to that narration and participate in the truth that [the text] tells."[29] There is no real hermeneutic at work in this model, or rather, the hermeneutic is "the realistic common-sense epistemology of the Enlightenment."[30] As Benedict XVI has said, the historical method has to let the biblical world remain in the past, and it oversteps its bounds to make it into something present today.[31]

The "text and its structure" without history is also problematic. Literature does not exist without some context. You cannot have a poetic witness without a referential witness. If the context is only the reader, then such a text with no external referent cannot tell the reader anything new.[32] If all the Bible contributes is the word on the page, then when one is faced with passages that appear problematic from one's ethical viewpoint,[33] the reader is forced to say, in effect, "I have a methodology that can make me the judge of Scripture."[34] Wénin, like John Milbank, fails to acknowledge that any quest for a contemporary theological interpretation for an ecclesial community ought to be interested in authorial and audience communities that theologically interpreted the text at its origin.[35] The blind alley of text without history was the project of the early twentieth-century Czech theologian Slavomil Daněk, and it

26. Räisänen, *Beyond New Testament Theology*, 111.

27. DiNoia and Mulcahy, "Scripture and Sacramental Theology," 343–44.

28. Dempsey and Loewe, "Introduction," xiii.

29. Hays, *Moral Vision*, 298–99.

30. Daley, "Knowing God," 19.

31. Ratzinger, *Jesus of Nazareth*, xvi, contra White, "Reflections on Isaiah 58:1–12."

32. Healy, "Behind, in Front of," 181–95.

33. Cf. http://www.godlessgeeks.com/LINKS/godkills.htm

34. Gregor, "Hermeneutics," 33.

35. Sargent, "Milbank and Biblical Hermeneutics."

both ignores the fact that biblical authors' intent sometimes was historiographical and risks losing the reader and his own story.[36]

But one must also question reading a text without any sort of canonical framework.[37] Roland Meynet's study of the Decalogue, for instance,[38] while making some valid and important theological points regarding the use of forms of the word ᶜ*ebed*, "servant," would take on completely new vistas if it were to interact with the use of that same term in Deutero-Isaiah and the figure of the "Servant of the LORD."

There are many questions, raised by Roland de Vaux in 1967, that this road still leaves unanswered.[39] First, which biblical tradition do we choose? They are contradictory in their theology.[40] As we have seen in Chapter One, the quest for a *Mitte der Schrift* is futile. Preuss recognizes this but tries to smooth out the diversity by seeking a "coherent whole," and "what is common" to most of the text.[41] Second, is this a theology, a theo-ology, "study of God," that is really a study of a textual God only, a character who depends on the Bible's testimony for an access point in the world?[42] Preuss explicitly says it is a theology "only as and in language,"[43] and Wénin seems to agree.[44] Finally, how do we distinguish between the text's theology and *Weltanschauung*?[45] Preuss's volumes appear, like von Rad's before them, like catalogues of the ancient Israelite worldview as it can be discerned from the text alone without the aid of

---

36. Sláma, "Beyond, Before and Within," citing material from Daněk, "Verbum a fakta Starého Zákona," 11–38.

37. Healy, "Behind, in Front of."

38. Meynet, "Two Decalogues," 1–35.

39. De Vaux, "Is it possible?" 56–58.

40. Murphy, "When?"

41. Preuss, *Old Testament Theology*, 1:8, 20.

42. De Vaux, "Is It Possible?" 56–58.

43. Preuss, *Old Testament Theology*, 1:24.

44. Wénin, "Analyse narrative et théologie," 48–56.

45. De Vaux, "Is It Possible?" 58–59.

archaeology. It is not a way to write the history of Israelite religion today;[46] it was never a way to write biblical theology.

46. R. D. Miller, *Between Israelite Religion*, 1–3.

5

Revelation in Canon
Brevard S. Childs and Other Originators

There is a branch of this first road, a variation on revelation-as-expression, and that is canonical criticism. Although he never liked the term, this method's father genius is Brevard S. Childs.[1] It began as a reaction in the 1960s and 1970s to the priority of history in the Biblical Theology Movement, which we will return to soon, and to the excessive concentration on the "original" (original Gospel, Q, J, etc.) in general.[2] The object was to interpret a text in the light of its biblical context—within the book and within the Bible.[3] On the one hand, this was an outgrowth of Redaction Criticism, on the other a return to the Spiritual Sense—each text within the single plan of God, arriving at a presentation truly valid for our time. So although, like Expression, canonical criticism rejects categories from dogmatic theology[4] and "turns on how well one can hear

---

1. Childs, "Interpretation in Faith."

2. Childs, *Biblical Theology of the Old*, 722.

3. For a discussion of how canonical reading works psychologically, see Lundhaug, "Canon and Interpretation."

4. Childs, *Biblical Theology of the Old*, 722.

and understand the biblical witness,"[5] it does so at the macro-level of the entire Bible, gaining theological insight from, for example, texts in the canonical order in which they were continuously copied over the centuries, regardless of dating.[6] In that sense, it is more than Expression, since the canon is supposed to show "the manner by which the hermeneutical concerns of the tradents left their mark on the literature."[7]

Childs was not alone in moving the locus of revelation to the canon. Rolf Rendtorff's canonical Old Testament theology was as massive as von Rad's was.[8] Dennis McCarthy looked "to the text as it is," reading "a single book with a unity."[9] Frank Matera has applied it to the New Testament, as has Margareta Gruber.[10] And authors ranging from Scott Hahn to Patricia McDonald to Dieter Böhler have embraced canon as a Childsean guiding principle.[11]

JAMES A. SANDERS

James Sanders's focus on canon as the locus of revelation originated independently of Childs, and there are important differences, although there are some similarities with Rendtorff. First, Sanders's canonical focus was more open to historical criticism than Childs's was. Sanders' interest was more historical, more interested in the

---

5. Childs, *Biblical Theology of the Old,* 41; Childs, *Biblical Theology: A Proposal,* 40.

6. Childs, *Biblical Theology of the Old,* 719; Childs, *Biblical Theology: A Proposal,* 41.

7. Childs, *Biblical Theology Proposal,* 40; see examples in Childs, "Reading the Elijah Narratives."

8. Rendtorff, *Canonical Hebrew Bible.* See also Rendtorff, "Canonical Interpretation"; and the method exemplified in Rendtorff, "'Covenant' as Structuring Concept."

9. McCarthy, "God as Prisoner," 34, 41.

10. Matera, "New Testament Theology," 20–21; Gruber, "Quelle zu Trinken Geben."

11. Hahn and Bergsma, "What Laws?"; McDonald, *God and Violence,* 32–33; Böhler, "Catholica et apostolica."

ancient "canonizing" communities.[12] Second, Sanders moved the focus from canonical literature, final form, to canonical process, a process he described as "monotheizing."[13] And Sanders means not only the process of canonization of the Bible, admittedly not completed until well into the Christian era, but the continuation of that same process "through Early Judaism into early Christianity and early rabbinic Judaism . . . but also each time thereafter that Scripture or tradition was re-appropriated so effectively."[14] Seen this way, "The canonical process . . . will not be complete until the eschaton."[15] He also envisioned this process as stretching backward to include "the first repetition/recitation in oral tradition."[16] As for Rendtorff,[17] for Sanders things are repeated over time in the canon, as tradition is contemporized (cf. Ps 78:1–10). At each point in this process, there is interplay of text, context, and reception; or logos, ethos, and pathos. That is, meaning is an interplay of the word, the reader, and the historical context, but this triangle exists in series, beginning with the earliest triangle when there was only oral tradition and continuing to today.

Though Childs was eventually willing to place emphasis on the canonical process, he restricts this to the "factors involved in the formation of the literature."[18] "The history of interpretation [merely] serves as a continual reminder . . . showing the *distance* between the biblical text and the interpreter and the degree to which the changing situation of the reader affects one's hearing of the text."[19]

---

12. Sanders, "Scripture as Canon," 58, 59.

13. Ibid., 60; Sanders, *Torah and Canon*, xxxi–xxxiii.

14. Sanders, "Scripture as Canon," 61; Sanders, *Torah and Canon*, 141.

15. "Scripture as Canon," 61.

16. Ibid., 62.

17. Rendtorff, *Canonical Hebrew Bible*, 717–39.

18. Childs, *Biblical Theology Proposal*, 39.

19. Ibid., 71; emphasis added.

SEITZ CHILDSEANS AND SHEPPARD CHILDSEANS

An odd situation exists among the students of Brevard Childs and the students of those students. As with no other model that this book will treat, the figure of the founding genius looms large over canonically focused hermeneutics, and so this "model," Sanders aside, is most explicitly the "Childs Model." At the same time, the arguments between Childs's students are fiercer than those between Childseans and those of completely different hermeneutics. Moreover, the argument often turns to who is truer to the methods and intentions of Childs, for example Christopher Seitz or Gerald Sheppard. Childs's other students, such as Randall Heskett and Stephen Cook, will weigh in their views on that question. It appears that Childs himself encouraged such behavior, for how else can one explain his dedication of his Isaiah commentary to "Christopher Seitz . . . defender of the faith?"[20]

The differences between Seitz and Sheppard-and-Heskett are significant, and in many ways, Sheppard addressed some of the problems inherent in Childs's work while Seitz has exacerbated them. But it will be easiest to see the different Neo-Childsean hermeneutics in the context of a discussion of the shortcomings of Childs and the questions his work raises. First, however, the positive aspects of Childs's approach, and that of Rendtorff and Sanders, should be enumerated.

That we do not have to recover previous texts, author's minds, or original audiences is a great plus.[21] The canonical method usefully expands with text-centered and reader-centered synchronic criticisms. It recognizes the inability to get "author's intent"—looking instead at "text's intent" in literary context. It eliminates problems of dating texts by circular reasoning and leap of faith and of basing theology on *Urtexte*. It is consistent with Scripture and Tradition (especially Augustine). After all, "these books did not come down to us separately but as a part of a collection."[22] *Ver-*

20. Childs, *Isaiah*.

21. Barr, *Holy Scripture*, 132, 139.

22. Brown, *Critical Meaning*, 32; Bouyer, *Meaning of Sacred Scripture*, 244; Scheffczyk, "Biblische," 197.

bum Domini 38 acknowledges the value of canon when it says that the progression from exegesis to theology "cannot take place with regard to an individual literary fragment unless it is seen in relation to the whole of Scripture," and certainly some theologians have used it precisely for this reason, as has moral theologian Lisa Cahill.[23]

Nevertheless, many questions arise. When is it justified for a theological interpretation to ignore such conspicuous complexity in the text?[24] That history of complexity is *part* of Scripture. Second, is it really irrelevant, as Childs says for the story of Elijah's contest with the prophets of Baal, how Baal was worshipped or what the significance of the choice of Mount Carmel was for the ancient audience? Would Stoic ideas of the *Logos* be irrelevant for understanding John 1? Without exploring historically "likely presuppositions, questions of against what opposing force the passage is written, and the like, interpretation would break down. Over many questions one would simply have to say one did not know what the text could mean."[25] Supposedly, there is no need for referents outside the text, but "the moment that one picks up a lexicon" he is being historical, as Heskett states.[26] Third, are texts prior to our current biblical text really immaterial? As Ralph Klein asks,[27] must we surrender the clear and poignant witness to truth in the Yahwist Source? Must we surrender the precious accounts of goodness that are emphasized by the Priestly Writer? Taking this even further, as James Barr asks, is the canonizing process always "right," always "a good thing?"[28] "Childs never considers that the canonizers might have been incompetent, or merely silly, or thoroughly misunderstood what the text was about."[29]

---

23. Cahill, *Between the Sexes*, 19–23, 31–33.

24. Barr, "Childs' Introduction," 16.

25. Barr, *Holy Scripture*, 169.

26. Heskett, "Deuteronomy 29–34," 37.

27. Klein, "Brevard Childs' Proposal," 108.

28. Barr, "Childs' Introduction," 13, 18.

29. Ibid., 18.

Seitz answers these questions by averring that Childs admitted there were prior sources, like J or P, but that biblical authors already moved beyond them in the redaction process. For this reason, we can see canonizers as scriptural redactors.[30] Seitz uses this notion in his analysis of the "Book of the Twelve," the Minor Prophets, drawing theological insights from the canonical arrangements of the books.[31] But the Minor Prophets are arranged differently in the Septuagint and the Masoretic text,[32] so Seitz is faced with a problem of which canon to consider "final"—part of a larger problem to which we shall return.[33] Childs concludes that the editorial devices inserted into the Minor Prophets identified by David Noel Freedman, Paul R. House, Paul Redditt, and others, suggest the Masoretic order is *the* canonical arrangement.[34] Among those editorial elements that suggest the order are the superscriptions, the opening verses that state in what kings' reigns the given prophet was active.[35] And yet do not those very superscriptions that Seitz says tie the books not to historical sequence but canonical sequence say to the reader that one is supposed to read the book that follows in the light of a given historical period?

Sheppard and Heskett work from the vantage point of the canon we have. For them, redaction and canonizing is not a conservative movement, since canon-conscious reading is innovation.[36] Sources like J or P, which they call pre-biblical traditions, are one level of abstraction, and then there is a biblical text, whose meaning is not wholly determined by the former level. We cannot focus authorial intent on the level of pre-biblical traditions,[37] but the canonizers do not mean to reconcile divergent views between

30. Seitz, *Goodly Fellowship*, 84–85.

31. Seitz, "On Letting a Text."

32. Sweeney, "Review of Seitz."

33. Seitz, "On Letting a Text," 162.

34. Ibid., 163–65.

35. Freedman, "Headings," 9–26.

36. Sheppard, "Canonization," 107.

37. Heskett, "Deuteronomy 29–34," 39; Deurloo, "Small Literary Unit," 44.

levels, a point to which we shall return, and so all levels are important.[38] In fact, canonizers used divergent views from multiple levels as an arena for theologizing. So neither does one level merely copy the one before in succession with only subtle modifications, as for Sanders,[39] nor does the last level negate all the others as for Seitz.[40] In Heskett's Isaiah example, Isaiah 7 must be read in the light of the entire book of Isaiah, especially chapters 9, 11, and 60–61. But this is not simply because we have a canonical book of Isaiah and so we must read it in its entirety, which was Childs's argument that was already superseded by Sheppard.[41] Rather, Heskett is aware that canon-conscious editing has taken place in the construction of the book of Isaiah itself,[42] so that Isaiah 9 is *already* in its written form a rereading of a prebiblical Isaiah 9 in the light of Isaiah 60–61, just as Isaiah 11 is in the light of Isaiah 40 and 65.[43] Seitz ignores the canon-conscious levels of traditions history, and for him, the theology only "kicks in" in the final form.[44]

Of course, there are still further questions for Sheppard and Heskett here. If I have to read Isaiah 9 in the light of Isaiah 61, why not read both in the light of Matthew? And if that is acceptable, how do we avoid issues of supersessionism? If it is not acceptable, on what basis? Boundaries of the biblical book of Isaiah? Boundaries of the Old Testament? Heskett does discuss New Testament uses of these passages, but does not bring them into the "meaning" of the Isaiah passages themselves. When boundaries between books and testaments are breached, there all sorts of questions that canon cannot answer. Did ancient canonizers mean to reconcile

38. Heskett, *Messianism*, 15–22, 39–59, 134–53, 225–37.

39. Heskett, "Deuteronomy 29–34," 45–46 n22; Sheppard, "Canonical Criticism."

40. Heskett, *Messianism*, 83.

41. Sheppard, "Book of Isaiah," 274.

42. Heskett, *Messianism,* 94. On this term, see Sheppard, "Canonization," 107 nn. 4, 6.

43. Heskett, *Messianism*, 98–131.

44. It is also probable that Seitz would only read Isaiah 65 in light of Isaiah 9, never the other way round.

divergent views?[45] *Verbum Domini* 39 says, "We see clear incon-
sistencies between them." John Barton asks, could a canonical
reading of James assure us that it does teach "justification by faith
in the Lutheran sense," after all?[46]

Let us return to other challenges to Childs himself. A most
basic problem is that there is no single canon,[47] and as Bartholomew admits, this "presents an enormous challenge to any
notion of biblical authority, vested as it is [for these scholars] in
a stable canon."[48] In spite of Childs's efforts to prove the antiquity
of the Masoretic Hebrew canon on the basis of Josephus, Philo,
and the Lucianic recension, "its most pristine and purest form,"[49]
we are confronted by the early Church's clear preference for the
Septuagint.[50] The differences are in both wording and book order
and in some books like Jeremiah these are enormous. On this issue, Seitz is obstinate: "The NT does not quote from a single LXX
text."[51] He denies the early Church preferred the Greek Bible.[52]

And there is more: as Carlos Bovell has pointed out, the New
Testament itself makes no distinction "between a primary, author-
itative" early Scripture "and a secondary interpretive tradition."[53]
Examples from James, Jude, and 1 Corinthians regularly cite as
Scripture what we would call Midrash or Pseudepigrapha.[54] Seitz

45. Blenkinsopp, *Treasures Old and New*, viii.

46. Barton, "Bible as Scripture," 10; also Lohfink, "Alttestamentliche Wissenschaft als Theologie?," 16.

47. Gerstenberger, *Theologies in the Old Testament*, 14; Petersen, "Review
of Seitz."

48. Bartholomew, *Introducing Biblical Hermeneutics*, 277.

49. Childs, *Biblical Theology Proposal*, 35; also Seitz, *Prophecy and Hermeneutics*, 150.

50. Schenker, "Die Heilige Schrift"; Ryan, "Textual Pluriformity"; Law,
When God Spoke Greek.

51. Seitz, *Character of Christian Scripture*, 73.

52. Ibid., 72.

53. Bovell, "Scriptural Authority," 20, 22; Smith, *Memoirs of God*, 169.

54. Bovell, "Scriptural Authority," 20–22. This continued into the Apos-
tolic Fathers. Rousseau shows that Polycarp of Smyrna similarly mixes what
we would call Scripture with other textual traditions and oral traditions and

again stands firm: there was a canon in place by the time of the New Testament, with only a small portion of the Writings still under debate.[55] Works like 4QReworkedPentateuch that seem to be "potential biblical books" even in the Law category are of no importance.

Moreover, one is left to wonder, as James Barr did, "What is the content of this theology?"[56] Even if canon is the sole guide to interpret the Bible for theology, this cannot say anything about God, salvation, etc. without taking a vantage point outside the text, which Childs deplores.[57] Seitz, in fact, admits this, and goes on to do it, taking a vantage point precisely that is outside the text: the rule of faith, in all its Trinitarian fullness.[58]

Finally, we must ask about authority and truth. Are the biblical texts authoritative because they are canonical—in which case we are back to Subsequent Approval[59]—or because they refer to something outside themselves?[60] Canonical approaches assume that the canonical Bible is "true."[61] John Barton asks, "Doesn't asserting that the self-revelation of God in Jesus surpasses what we learn of him from the Old Testament not imply that sometimes the Old Testament did not get it right, theologically?"[62] This does not seem to be an issue for Childs's students.

makes little distinction between them; Rousseau, *Early Christian Centuries*, 66.

55. Seitz, *Character of Christian Scripture*, 75; Seitz, *Goodly Fellowship*, 78.
56. Barr, "Childs' Introduction," 13.
57. Barr, *Holy Scripture*, 137.
58. Seitz, *Character of Christian Scripture*, 18–19, 171, 174, 198–99.
59. Poirier, "Canonical Approach," 366–70.
60. Smith, *God in Translation*, 30 n75; Barr, "Childs' Introduction," 16.
61. Barton, "Reading," 2.
62. Ibid., 8; echoing Scheffczyk, "Biblische," 198 n23, 199.

6

Revelation as Event

We finally move to a new road unrelated to Expression. Seeing revelation primarily as Event, this is the *Heilsgeschichte* or Salvation History model, which goes back to the Tübingen School of Johann Evangelist von Kuhn.[1] God acts in history with meaning.[2] Events and divine deeds reveal his character and morality for us.[3] God's revelation is in the history, his *Magnalia Dei* in the economy of salvation.[4]

The first major embrace of this hermeneutic was the mid-twentieth-century flourishing of the so-called "Biblical Theology" movement. Associated especially with G. Ernest Wright, this movement held that the way to produce theological insight from academic study of the Scriptures was to focus on *Heilsgeschichte* or Salvation History. God had acted in Israel's history, and those "mighty acts" were the locus of revelation. That is, the history described in the text, penned by the inspired community, *is* the revelation—revelation was not the "story of faith" but the actual

---

1. Kuhn, "Zur Lehre," 3–57.
2. Dulles, *Models of Revelation*, 53, 57.
3. Ibid., 55; Lemke, "Revelation through History," 34–46.
4. Dulles, *Models of Revelation*, 55.

events themselves.[5] For this movement, the problem of previous theological readings of the Bible was that they imposed anachronistic theological categories on the Bible. What was needed, instead, was a "theology of recital,"[6] which worked progressively in stages.[7] History has a meaning,[8] while "the Bible is thus not primarily the Word of God, but the record of the Acts of God."[9] Catholic exegetes and theologians were numerous in this Biblical Theology Movement. Pierre Benôit, John L. McKenzie, and Bruce Vawter speak of the *Heilsgeschichte*,[10] and Jean Daniélou states that "the Bible exists simply for the purpose of describing the *Magnalia Dei*: from Genesis to Revelation, it is nothing but a chronicle of these privileged events."[11]

In recent years, John Topel has repeated the view that the Bible "is about a God who acts in astonishing ways in history,"[12] and similar neo-*heilsgeschichtliche* models have been proposed by Horacio Simian-Yofre and Joel Green.[13] At the same time, a new wave in catechesis and the biblical apostolate in the United States focuses, even for adults, on "teaching people the narrative story of the Bible so they can understand the plan of salvation history," "looking at Salvation History unfolding throughout the Bible and recognizing that we are part of the story," "see how the plans, promises, and covenants of the Old Testament salvation history are realized and fulfilled," and so on.[14]

---

5. Stendahl, *Meanings*, 25.

6. Pythian–Adams, "Shadow and Substance," 420.

7. Ibid., 434; Dodd, *Authority of the Bible*, 229, 232.

8. Wright and Fuller, *Acts of God*, 17.

9. Wright, *God Who Acts*, 107.

10. Benôit, *Aspects of Biblical Inspiration*, 73; McKenzie, *Myths and Realities*, 62; Vawter; *Biblical Inspiration*, 161.

11. Daniélou, *Lord of History*, 149; cf. 157, 159, 165–67.

12. Topel, "Faith, Exegesis, and Theology," 338.

13. Simian–Yofre, *Assessment and Perspectives*, 289; Green, "Scripture and Theology," 18; Green, "Bible, Theology"; Green, "Modernity, History."

14. Bergsma, *Bible Basics*.

For the early adherents of the 1945–1965 Biblical Theology Movement, it was usually important that the events described actually happened historically.[15] Neo-Heilsgeschichtlichers are willing to focus on becoming engrossed in revelatory events that might not be historical.[16]

There are several points in favor of this road. It solves the problem of treating the final and terminal editor as the only inspired author or of "distributing the charism, so to speak, among the various men who contributed to the book" by making all the sources and redactors the heirs of a faith and a tradition that preceded them all.[17] It allows for a unity of the Old and New Testaments, based on "one divine action running through one history."[18]

It is consistent with Scripture (or at least J and Luke–Acts[19]) and Tradition (Ephrem, Bonaventure, Hugh of St. Victor). Gregory Nazianzus held that true exegesis is correlating the life of the believer with the ongoing economy of salvation (*Oration* 38.18); we must immerse ourselves in this history as if we too were primary actors in it (ibid.). In fact, this road has a heavy sway in modern Catholicism. *Dei Verbum* 3–4 adopted the idea that revelation consists especially in the acts of God, relegating the words to "proclaiming the works" (*Dei Verbum* 2).[20] *Optatum totius* 16 gives as the first of its ten principles a renewal of theology by contact with *Heilsgeschichte*. John Paul II, in his pre-Papal *Sources of Renewal* wrote, "The History of Salvation shows that God's action and the mission of the divine persons take place within time and in the sight of man and of humanity in the course of history, and

---

15. Pannenberg, *Basic Questions in Theology*, esp. 15, 19; Filson, *New Testament*, esp. 58; Wright, *God Who Acts*, 117, 123–24.

16. Topel, "Faith, Exegesis, and Theology."

17. McKenzie, *Myths and Realities*, 62–63.

18. Filson, *New Testament*, 64; Pythian–Adams, "Shadow and Substance"; Théobald, "A quelles conditions."

19. Tracy, *Naming the Present*, 53.

20. Norris, "On Revisiting *Dei Verbum*," 317–19; Fisichella, "Forty Years Later."

therefore become history themselves."[21] The method has been embraced by systematic theologians such as Leo Scheffczyk and moral theologians like Bernard Häring.[22]

But the main Biblical Theology Movement died dramatically in the 1960s and 70s. James Barr and Brevard Childs have been credited with its demise, but a host of biblical scholars shared their insights.[23] Most immediately, the Salvation History model fails to deal with non-historical material like the Old Testament Wisdom Literature.[24] One would have to ask Topel how exactly we "get caught up in the story" of the book of Proverbs, for example. "The Bible does not proclaim history as the only or even the main factor of revelation."[25]

The model lent itself to pious interpretations of reconstructed events, of which Phythian-Adams was a good example. The scholar reconstructed what *really* happened, and that was then interpreted theologically.[26] On the one hand, this required knowledge of history beyond the ordinary Christian's ken.[27] But what if historical evidence is contrary to the historicity of the events altogether? The landslide of sites and artifacts found in the ancient Near East in the last half of the twentieth century quickly eroded confidence in finding and recovering historical confirmation of Israel's narratives. It became what Leo Perdue called "the collapse of history."[28]

21. Wojtyla, *Sources of Renewal*, 157.

22. Scheffczyk, "Sacred Scripture," 28; Häring, *Free and Faithful*, 8–22.

23. Barr "Revelation through History"; Barr, *Semantics of Biblical Language*; Childs, *Biblical Theology in Crisis*, 13–96; also influential in the demise of *Heilsgeschichte* were Gilkey, "Travail of Biblical Language"; and Albrektson, *History and the Gods*. Bartholomew opines that reports of the movement's demise are greatly exaggerated; *Introducing Biblical Hermeneutics*, 362.

24. Dulles, *Models of Revelation*, 63; Barr "Revelation through History," 196.

25. Smith, *Memoirs of God*, 165.

26. Knapp, "Collective Memory," 123–24, 128; Billings, *Word of God*, 60.

27. Tracy, *Naming the Present*, 72.

28. Perdue, *Collapse of History*. Bartholomew is forced to rely on only the most conservative of biblical scholars and archaeologists to maintain a semblance of historicity even for the Patriarchs, to the point of appealing to the

Moreover, much of the model was built on a wrong (or tentative) chronology of Scriptures' genesis (what if the prophets are earlier than the Pentateuch, for instance?). "Salvation history does not appear to be so linear as *Dei Verbum* 7 depicts it."[29]

Who gives the meaning to history?[30] If it is the biblical writers, then this is the first road again. If not, then the interpreter is too powerful.[31] For Topel and Theobald, it is the community, to which we will turn in our fifth road.

The model leaves open what is to be our response to this history. Is it merely to be inspired? Topel and Green maintain it is to make ourselves identical with the original audience.[32] But this seems like a return to the Expression model.[33] In addition, and this is related to ignoring the non-narrative parts of the Bible which are also the most "ecumenical,"[34] as Benedict XVI writes, "Salvation history from a quantitative viewpoint almost disappears as a very minor part of world history. Whereas the totality of [world] history lives in an unseen manner from the brightness of the [biblical] light that comes from Israel."[35] In fact, if we allowed canon to be at all relevant we would have to recognize that historical narrative, particularly the Deuteronomistic History, is reinterpreted in Old and New Testament apocalyptic literature.[36]

Dennis McCarthy finds the entire model rooted in Hegel and Romanticism.[37] It owes much to the fact that "History has been and is the dominant (not exclusive) mode of perceiving experience,

---

long–discredited early readings of the Ebla Tablets by Pettinato; *Introducing Biblical Hermeneutics*, 363, 365, 367.

29. Lambrecht, "*Dei Verbum*."

30. Dulles, *Models of Revelation*, 56.

31. McCarthy, "Catholic Social Thought," 30–31. E.g., Filson, *New Testament*, 64.

32. Topel, "Faith, Exegesis, and Theology," 345; Green, "Scripture and Theology," 10; Green, "Theology, and Theological Interpretation."

33. Blondel, *Letter on Apologetics*, 269.

34. Brueggemann, "Triumphalist Tendency," 368, 374–80.

35. Quoted in Wicks, "Six Texts," 283.

36. Gresch, "Further Reflections," 88.

37. McCarthy, "Catholic Social Thought," 29.

searching for the 'real,' and structuring the self in the West."[38] I agree with the call thirty years ago of W. Taylor Stevenson, "that we cease to reifying history as a self-explanatory and self-evidently true and supremely privileged form of knowledge."[39]

38. Stevenson, "Myth and Crisis," 2.

39. Ibid., 12.

7

Revelation as Expectation

The fifth road emphasizes revelation as Expectation (*Auslösung*).[1] It is rooted both in Process Theology and in Anti-Essentialist Non-Foundationalism.[2] It sees interpretation as progress to new awareness, bringing a new inner experience.[3] As we expect the text to be increasingly brought into living intersection with our lives, the model is a forward-looking version of Revelation as History.[4] As in the inner experience model, faith precedes revelation.[5] There are no revealed truths in the text except those expressed in transient ways needing constant renewal, "inevitably disputatious."[6] Instead, the text itself reveals competing and complementary aims, testimonies and counter-testimonies as in a courtroom (e.g., the Deuteronomistic History vs. Job).[7] We cannot privilege one of

1. Dulles, *Models of Revelation*, chap. 7 and 199–201.

2. Brueggemann, *Ichabod toward Home*, 87–117.

3. Dulles, *Models of Revelation*, 99–101.

4. Ibid., 102, 104.

5. Ibid., 108–9. It is not entirely clear if "faith" is the right word; the important element is imagination as a subjectively used gift of the Spirit.

6. Brueggemann, *Book that Breathes*, 26; Brueggemann, "Biblical Authority," 13; Dulles, *Models of Revelation*, 98, 106, 109, 199.

7. Brueggemann, *Theology of the Old Testament*, xvi–xvii, 117–22.

these testimonies over another, but the interplay of them raises our consciousness and liberates our reason.[8]

Theologically, this road owes much to Pierre Teilhard de Chardin, for whom the text of Scripture was merely the starting point of the fullness of its meaning,[9] and to Edward Schillebeeckx, who declared the "manner in which revelation and scripture are heard again and again by man, *who makes history*, is precisely what is called 'tradition.'"[10] But it is also indebted to Anti-Essentialism and Non-Foundationalism, as in Walter Brueggemann's "anamnestic guerrilla theater," which envisions the text as a play performed anew many times in different contexts.[11] But these are not the new contexts of Sanders' process, they are key hermeneutical contexts supplied by the interpreter,[12] in Brueggemann's reading of Exodus 3, these are ancient Israel, the Passion of Christ, and Latin America.[13] "Theological exegesis is a rereading that has paradigmatic power in the future of the text."[14] Meaning of the text comes only by "this gradual growth in the community's awareness,"[15] until at last we are "listening to the one word of God here and now."[16] Inspiration "blows through the text in our hearing."[17] But this hearing is not interpretation of God's revelation; it *is* the revelation itself.[18]

---

8. House, "God's Design," 37; Dulles, *Models of Revelation*, 98.

9. Teilhard de Chardin, *Science and Christ*, 166–67. Such views sometimes led him to allegory: *Hymn of the Universe*, 59.

10. Schillebeeckx, *Revelation and Theology*, 176; italics original; cf. Brueggemann, *Ichabod towards Home*.

11. Brueggemann, *Ichabod Toward Home*.

12. Ibid.

13. Brueggemann, "Exodus 3."

14. Brueggemann, "Second Reading of Jeremiah," 168.

15. Schillebeeckx, *Revelation*, 173.

16. Ibid., 175.

17. Brueggemann, *Book that Breathes*, 33; Brueggemann, "Biblical Authority," 24–25.

18. Schillebeeckx, *Revelation*, 175; also Adam, *Making Sense*, 175.

Brueggemann writes, "We must not pay too much or primary attention to questions of history"[19] or even "reasonableness."[20] All readings of the text will be partial and tentative,[21] as "new participants" engage in "ongoing use of the text in the continued work" of "reusing."[22] Russell Pregeant said the same for New Testament interpretation: "every restatement is also by nature imprecise and analogical in the sense that all language can be so described."[23] Brueggemann believes that the New Testament's own freedom with the Old warrants our new creative, imaginative readings, each with the status of revelation.[24] Yet "the end point of the text has not yet been reached," Brueggemann writes. "The end of the reach of this text will not come until the last man or woman enacts courage and possibility."[25] In addition to Brueggemann and Pregeant, this seems to be the hermeneutic of Itumeleng Mosala, A. K. M. Adam, and Gustavo Gutiérrez.[26]

On the plus side, this hermeneutic is fruitful for calling man to help build the Kingdom. The moral theologian Josef Fuchs found it useful in making the Bible an "orientation."[27] It both allows for Sanders's canonical process and restores Tradition's Spiritual Senses. It is dependent on faith. It recognizes our own subjectivity in a way that other roads do not. It may be consistent with Tradition, as Aquinas observed, "Even the true prophets

19. Brueggemann, *Ichabod Toward Home*, 88.

20. Brueggemann, *Word That Describes*, 4; Brueggemann, *Interpretation and Obedience* 37–38; Brueggemann, *Creative Word*, 28.

21. Brueggemann, *Old Testament Theology*.

22. Brueggemann, *Ichabod toward Home*, 87, 99, 117; Schillebeeckx, *Christ*, 62–64.

23. Pregeant, *Christology beyond Dogma*, 43; cf. Schillebeeckx, *Christ*, 62. Kelsey questions whether Pregeant really presents a process hermeneutic; "Theological Use."

24. Brueggemann, "Bible as Scripture." Schillebeeckx, *Church*, 6–9. Hays is also fond of this "imagination" idea; Hays, *Moral Vision*, 298–99.

25. Brueggemann, "Summons to Holy Transformation," 169.

26. Mosala, *Black Theology in South Africa*, 173–93; Adam, *Making Sense*, 175, 182; Gutiérrez, *God of Life*, xiii–xvii.

27. Fuchs, *Christian Morality*, 13, 17.

did not perceive everything that the Holy Spirit intended in their visions, words, and actions" (*Summa Theologica* II–II, q.173, a.4). *Dei Verbum* 2.8 says, "There is a growth in the understanding of the realities and the words which have been handed down [from the apostles]. This happens through the contemplation and study made by believers, who treasure these things in their hearts (cf. Luke 2:19, 51), through the intimate understanding of spiritual things they experience, and through the preaching of those who have received through Episcopal succession the sure gift of truth. For as the centuries succeed one another, the Church constantly moves forward toward the fullness of divine truth until the words of God reach their complete fulfillment in her."

As articulated however, the model seems inconsistent with much of Scripture and Tradition, from Nicaea to the *Oath against Modernism*.[28] The model has little use for the canon or the Analogy of Faith, as Brueggemann writes, "We must not pay too much or primary attention to the settled theological claims of the Christian tradition."[29] The model's eternal progress into ever-better readings does not fit our experience; it leaves no room for the problem of evil, suffering, or sin.[30] David Tracy writes, "It is a history without radical interruption, without a memory of the victims of history . . . without Auschwitz, Hiroshima, or the Gulag . . . [It is] religionized narratives of some other story than the disruptive and disturbing narrative of the fate and resurrection of Jesus the Christ."[31] The model makes it difficult to find a use for the Bible (especially the Old Testament) and difficult to answer theological questions from it.[32] In fact, what one gets with Brueggemann are Brueggemann's readings, not a method one can replicate. This is why, although "It is difficult to overstate Walter Brueggemann's prominence in

28. Dulles, *Models of Revelation*, 111–12.

29. Brueggemann, *Ichabod toward Home*, 88.

30. Kropf, *Teilhard, Scripture, and Revelation*, 224.

31. Tracy, *Naming the Present*, 51.

32. Dulles, *Models of Revelation*, 112–13, 200; Childs, *Biblical Theology Proposal*, 58; Blondel, *Letter on Apologetics*, 277.

American OT studies over the past three decades,"[33] there is no Brueggemann school as there is a Childs school (or Biblical Theology Movement, etc.).

Can readings all be equally tentative? Is there nothing beyond the text (other than our own futures) by which to judge them?[34] Is even critical exegesis able to do this?[35] The text is, after all, concerned with history (the Pentateuch), with reasonableness (Proverbs), and with "settled theological claims." David Kelsey writes, "If a process theory of interpretation does not include a theoretical basis for judgments about what is normative (in this case for theology) in the texts being interpreted, then it is entirely unclear how a process hermeneutic is going to head off the truncation of theology whose roots in Scripture are not clear."[36] Brueggemann's Expectation readings leave us with only a courtroom full of testimonies without judge or jury. And if the text is repeatedly performed in the "anamnestic guerrilla theater," then as Kornelis Miskotte asked, "Wherein lies the power of the Scripture: to *lead* the spirits?"[37]

33. House, "God's Design," 35.

34. Ibid., 37–38; Collins, *Bible after Babel*, 146–47; Jensen, *Theological Hermeneutics*, 166–75; Davis, "Response to *Testimony.*"

35. Kropf, *Teilhard, Scripture, and Revelation*, 226.

36. Kelsey, "Theological Use."

37. Miskotte, *Bijbels ABC*, 27–28; English translation in Kessler, *Kornelis Miskotte*, 84.

8

Revelation in Ecclesia

As mentioned above, this road was not among Dulles's models. It goes hand in hand with what has become known as Post-Liberal, Narrative Theology. Hans Frei (1922–1988) provided the sustained theological arguments for narrative theology and George Lindbeck (b. 1923) then brought precision to it.[1] Independently, the "Amsterdam School" of Miskotte, Breukelman, and Deurloo promoted a similar approach, and so will be considered alongside the American "Yale School." And finally, this hermeneutic has been embraced by many in the "Emergent / Emerging Church" movement, which will also be considered in this chapter.

With regard to readings of the Bible, as Stanley Hauerwas writes, "narrative requires a corresponding community who are capable" of properly reading.[2] The locus of revelation, then, is ultimately this "community space."[3]

But there is also a positive circularity here in that the community is itself "story-shaped."[4] "The story of the church . . . be-

1. Robinson, "Narrative Theology"; Habets, "Dramatic Developments," 1.

2. Hauerwas, "Moral Authority," 243.

3. Huning, "Text, Life Situation and Faith," 10–11.

4. Bronsink, "Art of Emergence," 66, citing Rom 8:18–23.

69

comes hers through the narrative unfolding of Scripture uniquely experienced through the person and work of Jesus Christ."[5] Scripture, which Lindbeck calls the "paradigmatic graph," provides "native speakers" with a linguistic field of reference that is generative of a certain kind of culture, a certain way of being in the world.[6] "Practice, then, is the deliberate and unconscious physical manifestation of our story."[7] The words and deeds of God's revelation are brought to the Church "in a uniquely appropriate kind of narration in which a special way of remembering is actualized."[8] The community, thus shaped by the text, finds in the text "the traditions through which their community most nearly comes to knowing and being faithful to the truth."[9]

The community is not arbitrary, but is made up of those who share the historical (as with the third road) interpretive strategies of the texts' redactors, authors, and canonizers (as with the first road).[10] That community is "fundamentally identified and characterized by its story."[11] As Martin Kessler writes, "The secret of the church is that something exceptional happens: the Word."[12] "Practices themselves are lenses to the story . . . practices of remembering, rehearsing, and renewing," but, "The practices of the church are . . . gifts of the Holy Spirit."[13]

While Frei stresses the basic plain sense of the Scriptures, Lindbeck "characterizes the literal sense as that which a community of readers takes to be the plain, primary, and controlling

---

5. Ibid., 62.

6. Ochs, "Scriptural Logic."; Bronsink, "Art of Emergence," 63.

7. Bronsink, "Art of Emergence," 62; Lindbeck, "Search for Habitable Texts," 153–56; 154.

8. Miskotte, *When the Gods are Silent,* 197–98.

9. Hauerwas, "Moral Authority," 255; cf. 245, 259.

10. Metz, "Apology of Narrative," 89–91; Hauerwas, *Unleashing the* Scripture, 21.

11. Lindbeck, "Story–Shaped Church," 42.

12. Kessler, *Kornelis Miskotte,* 72.

13. Bronsink, "Art of Emergence," 63; Habets, "Dramatic Developments," 3.

signification of a text."[14] The text is stable and cohesive and received (contra Brueggemann), but the "story" is "not closed or finished,"[15] it is underdeterminate, it does not "have a meaning."[16] That is not to say that the text is anti-determinate, without semantic limits, with meaning all in the eye of the beholder, but that "interpretive pluralities" are possible informed by and congruent with the original purpose of the text. Nevertheless, one can never summarize the narrative in non-narrative form. Theology drawn from the text will be second-order reflections on how this Scripture sign-system is used in community.[17]

Stephen Fowl nuances this model by emphasizing the necessity of "being formed and transformed by God's grace in and through the friendships and practices of Christian communities . . . a lifelong process."[18] Communities avoid reading themselves into the text by taking their thick communal descriptions of God to be public truth, open to the judgment of the other.[19]

Fowl explains the role of the Historical-critical Method in this model, and it is a chastened, non-normative, and ad hoc role. The community's ability to read the Scriptures "over-against-ourselves" rather than simply "for ourselves" is "enhanced by ongoing engagements with critical scholarship."[20] "The practices of critical biblical scholarship are important to the ongoing life of Christian communities," "help[ing] Christian communities withstand their tendencies to self-deception in the reading of Scripture."[21]

14. Lindbeck, "Story-Shaped Church," 41; Habets, "Dramatic Developments," 1. Lindbeck's view draws on a "Wittgensteinian notion of linguistic meaning in which linguistic meaning is a function of language which varies according to the forms or cultures that users inhabit"; Habets, "Dramatic Developments," 4 n5.

15. Bronsink, "Art of Emergence," 62, 67.

16. Fowl, *Engaging Scripture*, 33.

17. Wisse, "Narrative Theology."

18. Fowl and Jones, *Reading*, 31; cf. 34–35.

19. Bronsink, "Art of Emergence," 65.

20. Fowl and Jones, *Reading*, 43. Cf. Fowl and Jones, "Scripture, Exegesis," 118–21.

21. Fowl and Jones, *Reading*, 40; cf. Lindbeck, "Story-Shaped Church," 49.

Positively, this road acknowledges the "hermeneutical circle" surely present in all cases, endorsing it as a beneficial element by reducing the subjective autonomy of the reader.[22] In so doing, it both appreciates Heidegger's insight that we grasp the meaning of the text only by appropriating it,[23] and allows for a harmonious relationship between Scripture and Tradition. This same "continuity of community" articulates a critical relationship between the two testaments based on history.[24] It appreciates the canon, based not on its received status but on unified theological conceptions.[25] The model is consistent with Scripture and Tradition, especially the etymological meaning of *Torah* as "catechesis" and *Dei Verbum's* views on the relationship of Scripture, Tradition, and Magisterium.[26] *Verbum Domini* substantially reaffirms this model when highlighting the "essential place in the Church's life gives rise to its genuine interpretation" (29). The modern life of the Church is the extension of the "faith traditions [that] formed the living context for the literary activity of the authors of sacred Scripture" (*Verbum Domini* 29). Building on the statement in *Interpretation of the Bible in the Church* II.A.2 that the authentic interpreter is "the person who has an affinity with what the text is saying on the basis of life experience," *Verbum Domini* 22 says that "only in this communion with the People of God can we truly enter as a "we" into the heart of the truth that God himself wishes to convey to us." Basil the Great emphasized that Scripture is interpreted within a believing community, what he called *hē tōn eulabōn chrēsis*. Bonaventure held that inspiration was "subject-inclusive": a believing subject was necessary for revelation, but the faith that actualizes

22. Hauerwas, "Moral Authority," 257; Hauerwas, *Unleashing the Scripture*, 21, 25; Habets, "Dramatic Developments," 3.

23. McLean, *Biblical Interpretation*, 305.

24. Lindbeck, "Story–Shaped Church," 45.

25. McCarthy, "Catholic Social Thought."

26. Kessler, *Kornelis Miskotte*, 62; Hauerwas, *Unleashing the Scripture*, 22.

Scripture is communal.[27] And like the inner awareness model, this road demands Christian actualization.[28]

The emphasis on narrative, however, easily "privileges the genre of story over against those other biblical forms of psalmody, law, and wisdom."[29] Although Lindbeck says that "a habitable text need not have a primarily narrative structure,"[30] he also holds that certain biblical texts have "the possibility of no application at all."[31] At the same time, the emphasis on (grand) narrative and the "something" (the Gospel) outside of the texts (e.g., the four Gospels) that they point to, might lead us to prefer some sort of "Life of Jesus" or Diatessaron to the Gospels themselves. We would lose the particularity of the four Gospels' unique voices in favor of the "story." And this particularity is important. Paul's letters to Corinth, for example, are revelation to the entire world but only by being "to Corinth" first.

If the community who best interprets the Bible is made up of those who share the historical interpretive strategies of the text's redactors and authors and canonizers, we are faced with the problem for the Old Testament of two such communities. Both Judaism and the Church claim this continuity with the biblical community.[32] Perhaps this Jewish-Christian problem could be avoided if defining the interpretive community moved away from such a *sola scriptura* description.

This road might support an anti-intellectual bias,[33] if, as Fowl writes, "the investigations pursued by people who do have such expertise, they are not necessary for wise readings of Scripture," which "requires that we develop specific patterns of acting, feeling and thinking well."[34] On the other hand, it is unclear if it matters if

27. Pidel, "Social Inspiration."

28. Hauerwas, *Unleashing the Scripture*, 49.

29. Childs, *Biblical Theology Proposal*, 59.

30. Lindbeck, "Search for Habitable Texts," 155.

31. Lindbeck, "Story–Shaped Church," 40.

32. Barton, "Preparation," 235–46; 239–42; Zenger, "'Gott hat.'"

33. Möller, "Reconstructing and Interpreting," 410–411.

34. Fowl and Jones, *Reading*, 29; also 33–34.

the "story" that shapes the Church is a historically accurate narrative or merely a story, which is one of the reasons why experts are not that necessary. But as we have repeatedly said, in spite of the exaggerations of the Biblical Theology Movement, in our historical faith God acts within history, not merely within a narrative.[35]

Lindbeck also says, "What God said in Scripture is not necessarily what he now says."[36] This is true, but one wonders how free of the textual mooring we can go. Lindbeck does say that the burden of proof is on those who would go against the text's historical meaning, but other advocates of this hermeneutic fail to recognize the need for the historical element of revelation to challenge the ideology of the interpreting community.[37] Moreover, since the Magisterium is rightly unwilling to proclaim the community's interpretation of every pericope, how is this not individual subjectivity?[38] And the alternative, as John Caputo points out, is "episcopal interpretation."[39]

Fowl is much more allowing of the text itself to speak, but nevertheless prioritizes the reader in hopes that we will "not cloud the issue further by calling the result of this interpretive activity "meaning" at the expense of other interpretive interests one might pursue."[40] Scripture unto itself, he writes, has no ideologies.[41] Lindbeck writes, "We have no definitively formulatable, context-free criteria for determining who is right and who is wrong."[42] How, then, do we let the text stand against us, challenge us, and remain other?[43]

Moreover, we are left to wonder if the Bible is normative for Christians because it is "our" text and we are "its" community, or

35. Batnitzky, "Biblical Criticism," 218.
36. Lindbeck, "Story-Shaped Church," 46.
37. Möller, "Reconstructing and Interpreting," 410.
38. Jensen, *Theological Hermeneutics*, 174–75.
39. Caputo, "Holy Hermeneutics," 204–207.
40. Fowl, *Engaging Scripture*, 58.
41. Ibid., 63–75.
42. Lindbeck, "Search for Habitable Texts," 154.
43. Batnitzky, "In Defense," 221.

if it is normative because it is true.[44] Finally, as Craig Bartholomew points out, in spite of much theoretical discussion, unlike the other models we have little application to date: "The fact remains, however, that there is little sign of this sort of biblical theology being written."[45]

44. Collins, *Bible after Babel* 135–42; Habets, "Dramatic Developments," 1.

45. Bartholomew, *Introducing Biblical Hermeneutics*, 76.

9

A Modest Proposal
Model of Revelation

The last road is the least clear—least clear, because it is my own road. I do not take credit for devising the hermeneutic model, but will lump a motley assortment of exegetes and theologians—James Barr, Norbert Lohfink, Raymond E. Brown, Hermann Gunkel, Sigmund Mowinckel, Hans Urs von Balthasar, Benedict XVI— together into a modest proposal I would like to put forward. What we ask of Catholic biblical interpretation is a new "actualization" of the text.[1] Much further work remains before specific procedures for this actualization can be enumerated.[2] Nevertheless, it is possible to outline a set of steps that would bring scholarly exegesis to a position of contribution to systematic (or moral) theology.[3]

My model does not fit well with Dulles's schema, his five elements of communication. Revelation does not consist primarily

1. Daley, "Is Patristic," 214.

2. But cf. Ignace de La Potterie, "The Spiritual Sense of Scripture," for suggestions.

3. Cf. Prior, *Historical Critical Method,* 236. The model draws on de La Potterie, *Hour of Jesus,* 151–54 which builds on Ricoeur. Farkasfalvy ("Case for Spiritual Exegesis," 342–50) proposed a similar model over twenty years ago, but none of these seems to have been seriously implemented by others.

of dialectic encounter, historical event, personal experience, written expression, or expectation. The content of revelation is, quite simply, God. This is a tenet of Catholic doctrine, affirmed also by Mowinckel, and it accords with Barr's view that revelation precedes Scripture.[4] *Verbum Domini* states, "The word of God precedes and exceeds sacred Scripture" (17.3). The Word, after all, "was God" (John 1:1),[5] and the Bible "points to a theological source or reality that lies *outside* the Bible."[6]

This conception relates to method because it allows a sequence where while the exegesis of Scripture precedes theology, that does not mean that revelation is something "added on" after exegesis. Moreover, revelation lying "behind" the Bible, not equal to its words or events (or symbols), is nevertheless contacted via those words, events, and symbols.[7] And yet, it is not contacted *only* by them; both Catholicism and Barr allow for—in fact, require—natural theology.[8] As will be explained below, this retreat from the *Sola Scriptura* that seems implicit in many of the above models (and Catholicism includes more than natural theology in its *Extra Scriptura* revelation),[9] relieves biblical exegesis of having to bear the full load of Christian doctrine, freeing critical scholarship to find out what the text really means.[10] It also eliminates the need to find a theological center of the Bible.[11]

My method begins with Benedict XVI's synthesis of Event and Expression. Exegesis must come first. That we must begin with the literal sense, a term I have hitherto avoided using for

---

4. Mowinckel, *Old Testament as Word*, 41; Barr, *Biblical Faith*, 196.

5. Also Pss 33:4, 6; 107:15; Isa 40:8; 55:11; John 8:27; 12:48; Col 3:16; 2 Thess 3:1; 2 Tim 2:9; Tit 2:5; 1 Pet 1:23; Heb 4:12–13; Mowinckel, *Old Testament as Word*, 43.

6. Barr, *Concept of Biblical Theology*, 494, italics original.

7. Barr, *Biblical Faith*, 196.

8. Ibid., 197 and passim.

9. Scheffczyk, "Biblische," 199.

10. Barr, *Concept of Biblical Theology*, 593–94, 602; Scheffcyk, "Biblische," 201; Lohfink, "Alttestamentliche Wissenschaft als Theologie?," 21.

11. Scheffcyk, "Biblische," 198.

reasons to be made clear shortly, has been maintained steadfastly since Aquinas (Thomas Aquinas, *Quodlibet*. 7, q.6, a.2, (art. 15), ad 5; *Divino afflante Spiritu*, 550; *Interpretation of the Bible in the Church* II.B.1). I have avoided using this term first because it is easy to mistake literal sense for "taking the text literally," which is not what it has ever meant. "At times they cannot be understood literally," as Gregory the Great said, (*Letter to Leander* 3), and Ephrem and Jerome would have agreed. "The literal sense of a passage is not always as obvious in the speeches and writings of the ancient authors of the East as it is in the works of our own time" (*Divino afflante Spiritu* 34–35). "Literal sense" is also problematic because it is easy to confuse it with the historical-critical method.[12] This confusing terminological problem can only be touched upon here. Thomas Aquinas rightly does not equate literal sense with authorial intent, but he does include in his literal sense some things that we now include under the term "Spiritual Senses"—the meaning expressed by the texts "when read, under the influence of the Holy Spirit, in the context of the paschal mystery of Christ and of the new life that flows from it" (*Interpretation of the Bible in the Church* II.B.2). We will talk about history shortly, and as we have seen, it is best to leave authorial intent to the side overall. We can, however, equate the literal sense with what Barton calls the "plain sense," "A semantic or linguistic and a literary operation,"[13] "what they can possibly mean, given the constraints of convention, genre, time."[14]

BIBLICAL EXEGESIS

I would propose calling the first step "Biblical Exegesis"; Ignace de La Potterie calls it the "Archaeological Approach."[15] This first step includes two movements. The first is literary exegesis, exploring the "language" of the divine-human communication. Here

---

12. Williams, *Receiving the Bible*, 26–33, 61–73.

13. Barton, *Nature*, 101.

14. Ibid., 113.

15. De La Potterie, *Hour of Jesus*, 151–52.

the scholar undertakes a philological investigation to understand (*Verstehen*) literary context, content, key words in the original languages, structure, genre, and other aspects of what is often inaccurately called synchronic criticism. It is really *Sprachgefühl*, linguistic sensitivity,[16] and it best proceeds according to the reading method of Tzvetan Todorov.[17]

The second movement of step one is the historical-critical method. For just as we cannot understand language without grammar, we have to use historical exegesis to determine (*Wissen/Kennen*) and grasp (*Respektieren*) the historical context, audience, situation, purpose, etc., the entire *Idiosincrasia*.[18] Even pre-biblical sources are important, as von Balthasar states, "Revelation, therefore, occurs partly before the Scripture."[19] Thus, Paul Joyce considers the first step to have three movements: words, context, and redaction.[20]

Even when the goal is theological, this first step is an independent work, propaedeutic to interpretation;[21] as Benedict XVI stated in a 2003 address to the Pontifical Biblical Commission, "the Magisterium no longer imposes norms on the exegetes from above, but they are the ones who determine the criteria that indicate the way for a fitting interpretation of this special book."[22] In *Verbum Domini*, no. 29, he reiterated, "This is not to uphold the ecclesial context as an extrinsic rule to which exegetes must submit."

16. Stolze, *Translator's Approach*, 178.

17. Todorov, "How to Read?"

18. Rae, "Texts in context," 40–41. For discussion of the latter term, see Gonzalez–Gerth, *Labyrinth of Imagery*, 15.

19. Von Balthasar, "Scripture," 3.

20. Joyce, "Proverbs 8 in Interpretation," 91–94.

21. Cantalamessa, *Mystery*, 89; contra Bowald, *Rendering the Word*, 170; and DiNoia and Mulcahy, "Scripture and Sacramental Theology," 338, although they seem to backtrack from their position on p. 344.

22. "On the 100th Anniversary of the Pontifical Biblical Commission: Relationship between Magisterium and Exegetes."

Step One is "independent" of the following steps in interpretation, but (contra John Collins[23]) by no means independent of the understanding of Scripture as inspired revelation. No interpreter ever fully prescinds from his or her presuppositions (*Interpretation of the Bible in the Church* III.D.11);[24] to deny having any is "a rhetorical strategy to dismiss other interpretations of Scripture."[25] Just so, the Christian interpreter does not prescind from his or her faith.[26] On the contrary, even these first, historical-critical steps, are acts of devotion (cf. John Cassian, *Conferences*, 14; *Divino afflante Spiritu*, 19),[27] which exist "in reciprocity" with theological hermeneutics (*Verbum Domini*, 35). Biblical criticism, writes Barton, "is no less religious than approaches such as the canonical one, but that it is actually more so . . . Prayer begins in attention to what is there, and then reflects on that 'thereness' in the light of religious convictions. But attention comes first."[28] "A critical approach is inherent in a religious commitment in the first place . . . An attitude of receptiveness to a reality we did not ourselves create."[29] But "the great value of historical criticism, from a Christian viewpoint, remains: that the attempt to do it forces us to pay attention to the text—to what it may originally have been intended to convey over against what we might want it to convey."[30] It allows us to read "Not constrained by prior convictions about the text's meaning . . . (which *includes* the scholarly guild)."[31]

23. Collins, *Bible after Babel*, 26, 33.

24. Pallesen, "Philosophy of Reflection," 44–62; Gadamer, "Problem of Historical Consciousness," 126; Ratzinger, "Biblical Interpretation," 7; McDonald, "Biblical Scholarship," 127.

25. Billings, *Word of God*, 8.

26. Thus Mowinckel advised to, "Seek first the kingdom of God, then come and receive clarity in theological–religious intellectual problems"; *Old Testament*, 21–22.

27. Anatolios, "Experience of Reading Scripture," 366.

28. Barton, *Nature*, 181.

29. Ibid., 186.

30. Bryan, "The Preachers and the Critics," 42.

31. Barton, *Nature*, 124.

INTRABIBLICAL HERMENEUTICS

Second, this should be followed by a History-of-Religions approach. Namely, we must look at the faith of Israel or the early Church *in* the Bible (not yet, at this point, a faith derived *from* the Bible), at what values underlie the text.[32] The goal is to "give a full account of the text which is an expression of religious faith."[33] Quite often, this expression is best seen in contrast to the competing ancient Near Eastern or Hellenistic milieu,[34] and there are examples in the work of José Severino Croatto on the early chapters of Genesis and a remarkably useful survey of this sort by Hermann Gunkel for the entire Old Testament.[35] This step is now hermeneutics, but an *intrabiblical* hermeneutics, and thus still "a certain kind of literal interpretation . . . basically still on the level of the '*historia*.'"[36] The problem with Road #1 is that it stops here.

These first two steps constitute a "background," which, in agreement with the Event road, has a progression or *taxis* (cf. Gregory of Nyssa, *Hexameron* 76, 86).[37] It is not so much a Salvation History, a *Heilsgeschichte*, as it is a *Traditionsgeschichte*.[38] But, as von Balthasar and Lohfink explain, the traditions of the Old Testament do not converge on their own, either by an overriding theme or by canonization, although each addition does involve a change in the meaning of the whole.[39] Nor is it correct to say they converge in the New Testament, since the New Testament focuses all interpretations of the Torah not on itself, but on Christ, and

32. Dulles, *Models of Revelation,* 194–95.

33. Farkasfalvy, "Case for Spiritual Exegesis," 343.

34. Smith, *Memoirs of God,* 166.

35. Croatto, "Tower of Babel," 203–23; Gunkel, *Water for a Thirsty Land,* 15–24.

36. Farkasfalvy, "Case for Spiritual Exegesis," 344.

37. Von Balthasar, "Word and Revelation," 234; Farkasfalvy, "Case for Spiritual Exegesis."

38. For discussion, see Nürnberger, "Evolutionary Hermeneutics," 4–10; and Nürnberger, *Theology of Biblical Witness.*

39. Bramwell, "Balthasar's Theology of Scripture," 315; Lohfink, "Über die Irrtumslosigkeit," 173; Barr, *Biblical Faith,* 196–97, 205.

since there are a number of elements in Old Testament faith that are never addressed in the shorter New Testament.[40] Rather, Christians read the Old Testament knowing the New, and therefore seeing a convergence on Christ not evident without such hindsight.[41] The convergence is not imposed by the Christian observer, it is merely only fully visible in such hindsight, from the right angle, but it was all the while "in the process of becoming . . . towards which it was steering from the very beginning," to quote Gunkel.[42] It is a "double organic" line "that proceeds through [both] *conscious break* and *conscious connection*."[43] The line of history, inspired oral tradition, authorship, and redaction, and *Traditionsgeschichte*—all of which together go into the "literal sense"[44]—leads forward, through Christ, to the Christian interpreter who is looking backwards in time along the same line.[45]

"One should regard everyone who made a real contribution to the wording and sense of a book as infallibly led by God with reference to the coming book, that is, as inspired."[46] Taking this to

40. Miskotte, *When Gods are Silent*, 262; Kessler, *Kornelis Miskotte*, 60; Nicholas Boyle, *Sacred and Secular Scriptures*, 89. Thus, for example, the Messiah, Daniel's Son of Man, and Suffering Servant are three distinct "characters" in the OT that never converge in that canon. The former two converge in the Book of Enoch, prior to the NT, while all three converge only in the NT, although the Trinitarian implications of the Son of Man are not clear until Nicaea. Cf. Farrer, "Messianic Prophecy."

41. Von Balthasar, "Scripture," 1; von Balthasar, *Glory of the Lord*, 408; Ratzinger, "Revelation and Tradition," 43; Billings, *Word of God*, 20.

42. Gunkel, *Water for a Thirsty Land*, 26; Lagrange, *Historical Criticism*, 65–67. Nürnberger argues that the Old Testament itself tells us what the central thrust is; *Biblical Theology in Outline*.

43. Mowinckel, *Old Testament as Word*, 31, italics original; Lohfink, "Alttestamentliche Wissenschaft als Theologie?," 15; Boyle, *Sacred and Secular Scriptures*, 86.

44. Ratzinger, *Jesus of Nazareth*, xxi; Farkasfalvy, *Inspiration and Interpretation*, 208–209.

45. Von Balthasar, *Glory*, 412; "Word and Revelation," 234; Mowinckel, *Old Testament as Word*, 107; Brown, *Critical Meaning*, 30.

46. Lohfink, "Alttestamentliche Wissenschaft als Theologie?," 166; Farkasfalvy, *Inspiration and Interpretation*, 211, 218. Bouyer shared the same view; see *Meaning*, 245, as did Koch, *Was Ist Formgeschichte?*, 111.

its fullest extent, then, Gunkel saw the non-Israelite ancient Near Eastern material drawn upon by the biblical authors as also part of this process, and it is difficult to escape this conclusion.⁴⁷ This is not the same as the Expectation/Process model, because the canonical text is still determinate, nor as the *Heilsgeschichte* model, because deeds are not privileged over words.

This means that what we call the Spiritual Sense, obtained as Lagrange noted by "collation, comparison, and development of biblical texts,"⁴⁸ is the last step of Traditions History (or, if you prefer, canon-conscious editing).⁴⁹ Michael Fishbane has shown that "Inner-biblical exegesis . . . reflects one part of a culturally integrated, 1000-year long spectrum of exegetical proliferation and development."⁵⁰ John Kutsko has argued that Jewish lectionaries predate and even set a model for the New Testament and that many texts of the Old Testament were liturgical and "lectionary" in their very composition.⁵¹ Recognizing "the liturgical function and form (genre) of certain texts from their inception and the incorporation into the ongoing liturgical traditions in Judaism and Christianity"⁵² connects historical Form Criticism with the canonical approaches of Sanders, Sheppard, and Heskett with the New Testament rereading the Old Testament.⁵³ It also "emphasizes the continuity between the earliest practices and contemporary practices,"⁵⁴ such as what falls under the rubric of "Reception History," to which we shall return.

47. Gerstenberger, "Cultural Breaks, Cultural Conformity." So, too, von Balthasar; Bramwell, "Balthasar's Theory," 319.

48. Schroeder, *Lagrange and Biblical Inspiration*, 26–27.

49. Von Balthasar, "Scripture," 11; Prior, *Historical Critical Method* 236; Yves Congar, *Believe*, 11.

50. Fishbane, *Biblical Interpretation*, 517; cf. 527–43; Sonnet, "Inscrire le nouveau," 3–17; Ratzinger, "Revelation," 43; *Jesus of Nazareth*, xviii.

51. Kutsko, "History."

52. Ibid.

53. Ratzinger, *Jesus of Nazareth*, 56.

54. Kutsko, "History."

Moreover, since "it belonged to the intention of the author . . . to bear witness to the divine economy, then it is in keeping with this intention to interpret the text as bearing witness in new ways to the singular divine economy in many different contexts."[55] Thus, the evolution of interpretations that produced the biblical text is the same evolution that we call Tradition.[56]

This is not to say that Scripture and Tradition are the same thing. For Catholics, the Bible, as *norma normans non normata*, is fixed and inspired in a way that the continuing oral and practical Tradition, authored by man even when the truth preached is the truth of Revelation, is not.[57] But the tracing of texts back to their historical origins and interpreting them in their proper historical contexts need not be seen as disconnected or unlike looking "at them in the light of the total movement of history and in light of history's central event, Jesus Christ."[58] As von Balthasar has noted, "It is not the organic character of history but the uniqueness of the Person of Christ, the God-Man, and his connection with his mystical Body, the Church," which necessitates Tradition.[59] "The witnessing Word is incapable of containing the infinite richness of the revealed Word, it means that there is always an overflow, which the Church receives as [a] vital . . . presence itself . . . then reflected back in the form of the Word which is the principle of Tradition."[60]

55. Rae, "Texts," 40; Ratzinger, *Jesus of Nazareth*, xx, where he ties this to Ricoeur; Barr, *Concept of Biblical Theology*, 585.

56. Farkasfalvy, *Inspiration and Interpretation*, 210; Legrand, "Fundamentalism and the Bible," 11; Jeanrond, *Text and Interpretation*; *Theological Hermeneutics*; Blondel, *Letter on Apologetics*, 270; Ratzinger, "Revelation," 44; Brown, *Critical Meaning*, 34 n.19.

57. DiNoia and Mulcahy, "Scripture and Sacramental Theology," 334.

58. Ratzinger, "Biblical Interpretation," 20.

59. Von Balthasar, "Scripture," 10.

60. Ibid., 11.

HERMENEUTICS PROPER

The "background" therefore, continues into the text's "foreground," which the interpreter must examine in what Benedict XVI called "a second exegetical operation"[61] and Barton a second "stage."[62] It is my Step Three. I call it hermeneutics; de La Potterie calls it "meaning."[63] Canonical methods as exemplified by Heskett are thus quite important here, "to let the total sweep" of the Bible "throw light upon and interpret the individual detail, even where this, historically speaking, is not the original meaning of the detail."[64] For the Old Testament, this third step also involves looking at a given text's use in the New Testament. In Christian interpretation, while "the whole economy of salvation . . . reaches into the future . . . and stretches backwards," von Balthasar writes, "the manifestation of the Word [Christ] constitutes the focal-point."[65] But, to reiterate, the "theological and spiritual trajectories of the Old Testament . . . [that] converge at the *telos* that is Christ, cannot be discerned on the basis of the *telos* alone.[66] The exegesis of a given Old Testament text must be allowed to unfold first [in steps one and two] according to principles and categories intrinsic to that text,"[67] but to read the Old Testament as if the New did not exist is to return to Fundamentalism.[68] Moreover, since Christianity is much more than a reinterpretation of the Old Testament (and Catholicism rejects

61. Ratzinger, "Biblical Interpretation," 20. Although I have used the terms "background" and "foreground" for several years, the terms have been used independently by Wilken, "Bishop as Exegete"; and similar terms are used by Schneiders, *Revelatory Text*, 127.

62. Barton, *Nature*, 165, 171.

63. De La Potterie, "Biblical Exegesis," 39–40.

64. Mowinckel, *Old Testament as Word*, 71; Rae, "Texts," 42; Barr, *Biblical Faith*, 196.

65. Von Balthasar, "Scripture," 1; cf. *Catechism of the Catholic Church*, 112; Aquinas, *Exposition in the Psalms* 21.11; Farkasfalvy, "Case for Spiritual Exegesis," 345.

66. Ratzinger, *Jesus of Nazareth*, xix; Billings, *Word of God*, 20.

67. Vall, "Vox Christi," 177; Ratzinger, *Jesus of Nazareth*, xix.

68. Gunkel, *Water for a Thirsty Land*, 26.

Sola Scriptura), this "line" described above cannot be the whole or sole path—it is more a line of sight.[69] The Old Testament does not need to bear the full load of a "Christian interpretation."[70] The principal of the Analogy of Faith is subordinate to the principal of the fullness of revelation being only in Christ, and so cannot dictate the meaning of the biblical text (of either testament).[71] And yet, at the same time, the ways in which the New Testament authors use the Old Testament are not altogether different from the ways Old Testament authors use other Old Testament texts.[72]

This foreground (de La Potterie's term) also includes "the entire history of interpretation."[73] Raymond Brown said, "A more sophisticated Catholic thesis would seek to trace a congruous development from the literal sense of Scripture to the church interpretation of Scripture."[74] But as Louis Bouyer argued well, that cannot "begin at the level of Christian antiquity."[75] Because of "the unity and the continuity of the people of God," "we must take the greatest account of traditional Judaism," the Pseudepigrapha, Merkabah mysticism, etc.[76] It includes the use of the text by the

69. Mowinckel, *Old Testament as Word*, 135; Scheffcyk, "Biblische," 200.

70. Barr, *Concept of Biblical Theology*, 242–44; see Heb 1:1. We can happily leave biblical truth in its *"fragmentarischen Charakter"* (Scheffcyk, "Biblische," 198 n.23) or *"Odium der Insuffizienz"* (Scheffcyk, "Biblische," 199).

71. Scheffcyk, "Biblische," 199. See Benedict XVI, "On the 100th," cited above.

72. Miskotte, *When Gods are Silent*, 231; Matera, "Future," 128; De Lubac, *Scripture*, 95, 118–19, citing observations of this already by Raoul of St. Germer (*In Lev.* 1.17, c.13), Bernard (*Sup. missus est*, h.2, n.11), Jerome (*Ep. 64*, n.20), Augustine (*In Pss. 113*, n. 4) and Origin (*De princ.* 1.4, c.3, n.13; *In Jos.* h.9, n.4; *In Gen.* h.10, n.5; *In Ez.* h.1).

73. Johnson, "Catholic Biblical Scholarship," 23; Barr, *Concept*, 581. While Murray Rae's method otherwise resembles mine, he fails to see the relevance of the diverse meanings of the text, the "particular meanings . . . in the divine economy," to *each other*, i.e., Tradition; cf. Rae, "Texts," 43.

74. Brown, *Critical Meaning*, 41.

75. Bouyer, *Meaning*, 243.

76. Ibid., 243, 244, 246–47; also Mowinckel, *Old Testament as Word*, 113. This is a serious flaw in the work of Lohfink; R. B. Robinson, *Exegesis since Divino Afflante*, 144–45.

saints and Doctors of the Church, in magisterial documents, in the liturgy, the lectionary, and the breviary—all of these sources read historically, not naïvely.[77] It includes these not only as representations of tradition, the likes of which shaped the text itself (as with the Revelation in Ecclesia model), but also as ongoing representations of that "pneumatic event" of inner experience, again, the likes of which shaped the text itself.[78] I am happy to emphasize with Räisänen that what is of value is the history of the effect of the text, not the history of it being muted—interpretations that would have taken a different course had the particular text not existed.[79] For examples of how to do reception history rightly, see the work of Ian Boxall.[80]

SCRIPTURAL EXEGESIS

However, contra Road #3, this is not yet the last step. The Biblical Commission's 1993 document says that the task of hermeneutics includes three parts:

> To hear the Word from within one's own concrete situation; to identify the aspects of the present situation highlighted or put into question by the biblical text; and to draw from the fullness of meaning contained in the biblical text those elements capable of advancing the present situation in a way that is productive and consonant with the saving will of God in Christ. (IV.A.2)

Raymond Brown called this, "biblical meaning as a whole";[81] I call this all Step Four and Scriptural Exegesis. It is de La Potterie's Teleological Approach and Farkasfalvy's Spiritual Exegesis.[82] It in-

77. Barr, *Holy Scripture*, 170.

78. Farkasfalvy, "Case for Spiritual Exegesis," 348; DiNoia and Mulcahy, "Scripture and Sacramental Theology," 335; Rae, "Texts," 41.

79. Räisänen, "Effective 'History' of the Bible," 311–15; Cantalamessa, *Mystery*, 49.

80. Boxall, "Reception History"; *Patmos in Reception History*.

81. Brown, *Critical Meaning*, 20.

82. De La Potterie, *Hour*, 151, 153–54; Cantalamessa, *Mystery*, 86;

cludes the "Ecclesia" road's reading in community.[83] To interrelate our text with contemporary experience, vocabulary, and religious impact, it is not enough to homilize. It is academic theology that reflects critically on the intersection between the contemporary situation and the content of faith, and so the text, now enriched by background and foreground, needs to intersect with theology.[84] We need to examine ways in which modern theologians (Catholic and Protestant) appropriate the text's "symbols."

The interpreter now proposes a valid recontextualization of the text.[85] This completes the bridging of the theological gap and offers a new actualization. The exegete has now "elucidated the treasure of light and life contained in the Sacred Scriptures" (see above), and become a part of "the drama of divine revelation itself."[86] John Barton admits, "This has happened patchily, but still to a significant extent, in biblical studies."[87] He writes, "My own conviction is that this is because hardly anyone has ever tried."[88]

CRITICISM OF THE MODEL

It would be arrogant to omit any criticism of this last model. The weaknesses that are clear to me all concern the *taxis*, the line of development that stretches from ancient Near Eastern material to pre-biblical texts like J, to the Old Testament and its own intertextuality, to the New Testament, and finally through two thousand years of reception history. It is not my intent to leave the formation of Scripture merely one incidental phase in this *taxis*.[89] As I

Farkasfalvy, "Case for Spiritual Exegesis." Cf. Joyce, "Proverbs 8," 96–101.

83. Mowinckel, *Old Testament as Word of God*, 126.

84. Ibid., 126–27.

85. Jensen, *Theological Hermeneutics,* chap. 13; Mowinckel, *Old Testament as Word*, 132; Schökel, *Il dinamismo della tradizione*, 276.

86. Jason Bourgeois, "Balthasar's Theodramatic Hermeneutics," 128; Kurz, *Future*, 150.

87. Barton, *Nature*, 177, 180.

88. Ibid., 190.

89. A warning from Heskett, *Messianism*, 273.

have stated, it is the *norma normans*, but I recognize that given the abundance of data that my method would entail, it would be easy for the actual biblical witness to be given no more attention than any other phase, and perhaps less attention since the Bible is bound to be more familiar than either the ancient Near Eastern material or a given patristic interpretation.

The second danger concerning this *taxis* is whether calling it a line at all amounts to "a pious accounting for all the changes."[90] I did say that the line cannot be the only line or sole path, but Benedict XVI is stronger: it "is certainly not linear."[91] Heskett is quite wary of such "lines," and says, "My approach does not attempt to locate lines of continuity or even trajectories."[92] And yet Heskett does trace a progression from traditions history to redaction to canonization.[93] The key will be to hold on to the discontinuities, as Joyce does, using them as spurs to imaginative but text-centered interpretation, and focus on what tradition has moved on to the next period in time and text.[94]

Third, should we be wary if it were possible for any scholar, Jewish, Buddhist, atheist, to trace the same *taxis* that I am proposing? Could not anyone line up the pre-biblical background, sound exegesis, and *Wirkungsgeschichte*?[95] And if so, is that a problem? My own sense is that in many ways, such a scholar could do so, but I am not sure it is a problem. Isn't part of the point of our understanding of inspiration that the text is not an "insiders-only" sort of thing? One doesn't have to be initiated to read it, or even to be enlightened by it, and notable readers of it like St. Paul, Nicholas of Lyra, and Charles Péguy come to mind as illustrations.

Perhaps the key question is not "is it possible," "is it possible for a scholar who is not a part of the Ecclesia to bring higher

90. Heskett, *Messianism*, 273.

91. Benedict, *Jesus of Nazareth*, xix.

92. Heskett, *Messianism*, 265.

93. Ibid., 266.

94. Joyce, "First among Equals," 23, 26; Nürnberger, *Theology of Biblical Witness*, 115–33; Nürnberger, *Biblical Theology*, 65–67.

95. Farrer, "Images and Inspiration," 29.

criticism to the theologian for it to form the foundation of their own work, to bring exegesis to theology?" That is the problem this book set out to address, and it might be possible. They key question regarding the faith of the interpreter, rather, must move us beyond the scope of this book entirely. The full response to revelation is faith (Benedict XVI, *Verbum Domini* 25). John Paul II wrote, "The response to revelation is not simply a matter of intellectually accepting its content but . . . an attitude in which man freely commits his entire self to God."[96] Human communication occurs primarily in conversation, and a monologue from God is not likely to continue. True revelation is achieved only through the life to which the Logos-made-flesh calls us.

21st century
no - isms - sex
paternalism

96. Wojtyla, *Sources of Renewal*, 53–54.

Bibliography

Abraham, William J. "The Authority of Scripture and the Birth of Biblical Theology." *Journal of Theology* 3 (2007) 3–13.

Adam, A. K. M. *Making Sense of New Testament Theology.* Studies in American Biblical Hermeneutics 11. Macon, GA: Mercer University Press, 1995.

Albrektson, Bertil. *History and the Gods: An Essay on the Idea of Historical Events as Divine Manifestations in the Ancient Near East and in Israel.* Coniectanea biblica: Old Testament Series 1. 1967. Reprinted, Winona, IN: Eisenbrauns, 2011.

Alonso Schökel, Luis. *Il dinamismo della tradizione.* Brescia: Paideia, 1970.

———. *The Inspired Word: Scripture in the Light of Language and Literature.* Translated by Francis Martin. New York: Herder & Herder, 1965.

———. *A Manual of Hermeneutics.* Translated by Liliana M. Rosa. Biblical Seminar 54. Sheffield: Sheffield Academic, 1998.

Anatolios, Khaled. "Inspiration and the Fecundity of Scripture." Paper presented at the conference "*Dei Verbum* at 50: Toward a Clarification of the Inspiration of Scripture." Dayton, 2012.

———. "The Experience of Reading Scripture in the Early Christian Tradition." *Fides Quaerens Intellectum* 1 (2001) 359–70.

Balthasar, Hans Urs von. *The Glory of the Lord: A Theological Aesthetics.* Translated by Erasmo Leiva-Merikakis. Edited by Joseph Fessio and John Riches. San Francisco: Ignatius, 1991.

———. "Scripture as the Word of God." *Downside Review* 68 (1950) 1–20.

———. "Word and Revelation." In *Sacred Scripture,* edited by James J. Megivern. 2:217–38. The Catholic Tradition 8. Wilmington, NC: McGrath, 1979.

Barr, James. *Biblical Faith and Natural Theology.* Oxford: Oxford University Press, 1993.

———. "Childs' Introduction to the Old Testament." *JSOT* 16 (1980) 12–23.

———. *The Concept of Biblical Theology: An Old Testament Perspective.* Minneapolis: Fortress, 1999.

———. *Holy Scripture: Canon, Authority, Criticism.* Philadelphia: Westminster, 1983.

———. "Revelation through History in the Old Testament and in Modern Theology." *Interpreation* 17 (1963) 193–205.

———. *The Semantics of Biblical Language.* London: Oxford University Press, 1961.

Barth, Karl. *Church Dogmatics* I/2, *The Doctrine of the Word of God.* Edited by G. W. Bromiley and T. F. Torrance. Translated by G. T. Thomson and Harold Knight. Edinburgh: T. & T. Clark, 1956.

Barton, John. *The Nature of Biblical Criticism.* Louisville: Westminster John Knox, 2007.

———. "Preparation in History for Christ." In *The Old Testament: Canon, Literature, and Theology,* edited by John Barton, 235–46. Burlington, VT: Ashgate, 2007.

———. "Reading the Bible as Scripture." Paper presented to the Irish Biblical Association Annual Conference. Dublin, 2006.

Batnitzky, Leora. "In Defense of Biblical Criticism." *Hebraic Political Studies* 4 (2009) 212–21.

Bea, Augustin. "Inspiration et Révélation." In *Supplément Dictionnaire de la Bible* 4:504–5. Paris: Letouzey & Ané, 1948.

Bell, Allan. "Re-constructing Babel: Discourse Analysis, Hermeneutics and the Interpretive Arc." *Discourse Studies* 13 (2001) 519–68.

Bellamah, Timothy. "Late Medieval Perspectives on History, Authority and Authorial Intention." Paper presented at the conference: "*Dei Verbum* at 50: Toward a Clarification of the Inspiration of Scripture." Dayton, 2012.

Benedict XVI. "Easter Vigil Homily." April 23, 2011.

———. "Message to Participants in the Plenary Meeting of the Pontifical Biblical Commission." May 2, 2011.

Benôit, Pierre. *Aspects of Biblical Inspiration.* Translated by J. Murphy-O'Connor and S. K. Ashe. Probe Books. Chicago: Priory, 1965.

Bergant, Dianne. *Job, Ecclesiastes.* Old Testament Message 18. Wilmington, DE: Glazier, 1982.

———. *People of the Covenant: An Invitation to the Old Testament.* Come & See. Franklin, WI: Sheed & Ward, 2001.

Bergsma, John. *Bible Basics for Catholics: A New Picture of Salvation History.* Notre Dame: Ave Maria, 2012.

Billings, J. Todd. *The Word of God for the People of God: An Entryway to the Theological Interpretation of Scripture.* Grand Rapids: Eerdmans, 2010.

Blenkinsopp, Joseph. *Treasures Old and New: Essays in the Theology of the Pentateuch.* Grand Rapids: Eerdmans, 2004.

Blondel, Maurice. *Letter on Apologetics; and History and Dogma.* Translated by Alexander Dru and Illtyd Trethowan. Ressourcement. New York: Rinehart & Winston, 1965.

Boadt, Lawrence. *Reading the Old Testament: An Introduction.* Mahwah, NJ: Paulist, 1984.

Böhler, Dieter, SJ. "Catholica et apostolica—die Kirche in der Hl. Schrift." *Philosophisch-Theologische Hochschule Sankt Georgen Virtueller Leseraum.* http://www.sankt-georgen.de/leseraum/boehler4.pdf.

Bonfrère, Jacques. *Pentateuchis Mosis commentario illustatis, praemissis praeloquiis perutilibus.* Antwerp, 1625.

Bourgeois, Jason. "Balthasar's Theodramatic Hermeneutics." In *Theology and Sacred Scripture,* edited by Carol J. Dempsey and William P Loewe, 125–34. College Theology Society Annual 47. Maryknoll, NY: Orbis, 2002.

Bouyer, Louis. *The Meaning of Sacred Scripture.* Translated by Mary Perkins Ryan. Liturgical Studies 5. Notre Dame: Notre Dame University Press, 1958.

———. "Où en est le mouvement biblique?" *Bible et Vie chrétienne* 13 (1956) 7–21.

Bovell, Carlos. "All Scripture Is Hermeneutically God–Breathed." In *Biblical Inspiration and the Authority of the Bible: Suggestions for a Believable Doctrine of Scripture for the 21st Century,* edited by Carlos Bovell, 3–26. Eugene, OR: Wipf & Stock, 2014.

———. "Scriptural Authority and Believing Criticism." *Journal of Philosophy and Scripture* 3 (2005) 17–27.

Bowald, Mark Alan. *Rendering the Word in Theological Hermeneutics: Mapping Divine and Human Agency.* Farnham, VT: Ashgate, 2007.

Boxall, Ian. *Patmos in the Reception History of the Apocalypse.* Oxford: Oxford University Press, 2013.

———. "Reception History." In *The New Cambridge History of the Bible,* edited by John Riches, 4:172–83. Cambridge: Cambridge University Press, 2014.

Boyle, Nicholas. *Sacred and Secular Scriptures: A Catholic Approach to Literature.* London: Darton, Longman & Todd, 2004.

Bramwell, Bevil. "Hans Urs von Balthasar's Theology of Scripture." *New Blackfriars* 86 (2005) 308–22.

Breck, Jean. "Verite et Sens dans les Saintes Ecritures." *Service Biblique Catholique* (blog). http://www.bible–service.net/extranet/current/pages/846.html

Bright, John. *Early Israel in Recent History Writing: A Study in Method.* Studies in Biblical Theology 1/19. London: SCM, 1960.

Bronsink, Troy. "The Art of Emergence: Being God's Handiwork." In *An Emergent Manifesto of Hope,* edited by Doug Pagitt and Tony Jones, 59–74. Grand Rapids: Baker, 2007.

Brown, Rayond E. *The Critical Meaning of the Bible.* New York: Paulist, 1981.

Brueggemann, Walter. "The Bible as Scripture Canon Fire." *Christian Century* 5 (2001) 22–26.

———. "Biblical Authority: A Personal Reflection." In *Struggling with Scripture,* by Walter Brueggemann, William Carl Placher, and Brian K. Blount, 5–31. Louisville: Westminster John Knox, 2002.

———. *The Book that Breathes New Life: Scriptural Authority and Biblical Theology.* Minneapolis: Fortress, 2005.

———. *The Creative Word: Canon as a Model for Biblical Education.* Minneapolis: Fortress, 1982.

———. "Exodus 3: Summons to Holy Transformation." In *The Theological Interpretation of Scripture,* edited by Steven E. Fowl, 155–72. Oxford: Blackwell, 1997.

———. *Ichabod Toward Home: The Journey of God's Glory.* 2002. Reprinted, Eugene, OR: Wipf & Stock 2005.

———. *Interpretation and Obedience: From Faithful Reading to Faithful Living.* Minneapolis: Fortress, 1991.

———. *Old Testament Theology: Essays on Structure, Theme, and Text.* Minneapolis: Fortress, 1992.

———. "A Second Reading of Jeremiah after the Dismantling." *Ex Auditu* 1 (1985) 156–68.

———. *Theology of the Old Testament: Testimony, Dispute, Advocacy.* Minneapolis: Fortress, 2012.

———."The Triumphalist Tendency in Exegetical History." *JAAR* 38 (1970) 367–80.

———. *The Word That Describes the World: The Bible and Discipleship.* Minneapolis: Fortress, 2006.

Bryan, Christopher. "The Preachers and the Critics: Thought on Historical Criticism." *Anglican Theological Review* 74 (1991) 37–53.

Bühler, Karl. *Die geistige Entwicklung des Kindes.* 3rd ed. Jena: Fischer, 1922.

Bush, Tom. "Sola Scriptura in Catholic Seminaries." *Homiletic and Pastoral Review* 100.4 (2000) 31–32.

Cahill, Lisa. *Between the Sexes: Foundations for a Christian Ethics of Sexuality.* Philadelphia: Fortress, 1985.

Caird, G. B. *New Testament Theology.* Completed and edited by L. D. Hurst. Oxford: Clarendon, 1994.

Cantalamessa, Raniero. *The Mystery of God's Word.* Translated by Alan Neame. Collegeville, MN: Liturgical, 1994.

Caputo, John D. "Holy Hermeneutics versus Devilish Hermeneutics: Textuality and the Word of God." In *More Radical Hermeneutics: On Not Knowing Who We Are,* 193–219. Studies in Continental Thought. Bloomington: Indiana University Press, 2000.

Chapp, Larry S. *The God Who Speaks: Hans Urs von Balthasar's Theology of Revelation.* San Francisco: International Scholars Publications, 1996.

Cheyne, T. K. *The Hallowing of Criticism: Nine Sermons on Elijah Preached in Rochester Cathedral, with an Essay Read at the Church Congress, Manchester, October 2nd, 1888.* London: Hodder & Stoughton, 1888.

Childs, Brevard S. *Biblical Theology: A Proposal.* Facets. Minneapolis: Fortress, 2002.

———. *Biblical Theology in Crisis.* Philadelphia: Westminster, 1970.

———. "Interpretation in Faith: The Theological Responsibility of an Old Testament Commentary." *Int* 18 (1964) 432–49.

———. *Isaiah.* OTL. Louisville: Westminster John Knox, 2001.

————. "Reading the Elijah Narratives." *Int* 34 (1980) 128–37.

————. *Theology of the Old and New Testaments: Theological Reflections on the Christian Bible.* Minneapolis: Fortress, 1992.

Claudel, Paul. *The Essence of the Bible.* New York: Philosophical Library, 1957.

Collins, John J. *Encounters with Biblical Theology.* Minneapolis: Fortress, 2005.

————. *The Bible after Babel: Historical Criticism in a Postmodern Age.* Grand Rapids: Eerdmans, 2006.

Congar, Yves. *I Believe in the Holy Spirit.* New York: Crossroad Herder, 1997.

Conzelmann, Hanz. *An Outline of the Theology of the New Testament.* Translated by John Bowden. New York: Harper & Row, 1969.

Croatta, J. Severino. "A Reading of the Tower of Babel from the Perspective of Non-Identity." In *Teaching the Bible: The Discourses and Politics of Biblical Pedagogy*, edited by Fernando F. Segovia and Mary Ann Tolbert, 203–23. Maryknoll, NY: Orbis, 1998.

Curran, Charles E. "The Role and Function of the Scriptures in Moral Theology." In *The Use of Scripture in Moral Theology*, edited by Charles E. Curran and Richard A. McCormick, 178–214. Readings in Moral Theology 4. New York: Paulist, 1984.

————. *Themes in Fundamental Moral Theology.* Notre Dame: Notre Dame University Press, 1977.

D'Hulst, Maurice Le Sage d'Hauteroche. "La Question Biblique." *Le Correspondant*, Jan 25, 1893.

Daley, Brian E. "Is Patristic Exegesis Still Usable?" *Communio* 29 (2002) 185–216.

————. "Knowing God in History and in the Church: *Dei Verbum* and 'Nouvelle Théologie'." Presentation to the United States Conference of Catholic Bishops on the 40th Anniversary of *Dei Verbum.* Chicago, 2005.

————. "La Nouvelle Theologie and the Patristic Revival: Sources, Symbols, and the Science of Theology." *IJST* 7 (2005) 362–82.

Daněk, Slavomil C. "Verbum a fakta Starého Zákona." *Ročenka Husovy Fakulty*, (1937) 11–38.

Daniélou, Jean. *The Lord of History.* Translated by Nigel Abercrombie. Cleveland: World, 1968.

Davis, Ellen F. "A Response to *Theology of the Old Testament: Testimony, Dispute, Advocacy* by Walter Brueggemann." *Virginia Seminary Journal* (July 1999) 49–54.

Deurloo, K.A. "The Scope of a Small Literary Unit in the Old Testament." In *Voices from Amsterdam: A Modern Tradition of Reading Biblical Narrative*, edited by Martin Kessler, 37–51. Semeia Studies. Atlanta: Society of Biblical Literature, 1994.

Dempsey, Carol J., and William P. Loewe. "Introduction." In *Theology and Sacred Scripture*, xi–xv. Annual Publication of the College Theology Society 47. Maryknoll, NY: Orbis, 2002.

DiNoia, J. A., and Bernard Mulcahy. "The Authority of Scripture in Sacramental Theology." *Pro Ecclesia* 10 (2001) 329–45.

Dodd, C.H. *The Authority of the Bible.* London: Fontana, 1971.

Donahue, John R. *The Gospel in Parable: Metaphor, Narrative, and Theology in the Synoptic Gospels.* Philadelphia: Fortress, 1988.

Dulles, Avery. *Models of Revelation.* New York: Orbis, 1992.

———. *Revelation Theology.* New York: Herder and Herder, 1969.

———. "Scripture and Magisterium in *Dei Verbum.*" Presentation to the United States Conference of Catholic Bishops on the 40th Aniversary of *Dei Verbum*, Chicago, 2005.

———. "Symbol, Myth, and the Biblical Revelation." *Theological Studies* 27 (1966) 1–26.

———. "Theology in Priestly Formation." Address to the International Institute for Clergy Formation Summer Institute for Priests, 2005.

Eichrodt, Walter. *Theology of the Old Testament.* Philadelphia: Westminster, 1961.

Enns, Peter. *Inspiration and Incarnation.* Grand Rapids: Baker, 2005.

Farkasfalvy, Denis. "How to Complete *Dei Verbum.*" Paper presented at the conference "*Dei Verbum* at 50: Toward a Clarification of the Inspiration of Scripture." Dayton, 2012.

———. "Inspiration and Incarnation." Paper presented at the 1st Monsignor Jerome D. Quinn Conference: "The Word of God in the Life and Ministry of the Church." St. Paul, 2009.

———. *Inspiration and Interpretation.* Washington, DC: Catholic University of America Press, 2010.

———. "The Case for Spiritual Exegesis." *Communio* 10 (1983) 332–50.

Farrer, Austin. "Images and Inspiration." In *The Truth Seeking Heart*, Canterbury Studies in Spiritual Theology 3, edited by A. Loades and R. MacSwain. 20–36. Norwich: Canterbury, 2006.

———. "Messianic Prophecy." In *The Truth-Seeking Heart: Austin Farrer and His Writings*, edited by Ann Loades and Robert MacSwain, 37–46. Canterbury Studies in Spiritual Theology 3. Norwich: Canterbury, 2006.

Filson, Floyd. *The New Testament against Its Environment.* Studies in Biblical Theology 1/3. London: SCM, 1950.

Fisichella, Rino. "*Dei Verbum* Forty Years Later." Presentation to the United States Conference of Catholic Bishops on the 40th Anniversary of *Dei Verbum*. Chicago, 2005.

Fishbane, Michael. *Biblical Interpretation in Ancient Israel.* Oxford: Clarendon, 1985.

Fitzmyer, Joseph. *Scripture the Soul of Theology.* New York: Paulist, 1994.

Fletcher, Joseph. *Situation Ethics: The New Morality.* Louisville: Westminster John Knox, 1966.

Fowl, Stephen E. *Engaging Scripture: A Model for Theological Interpretation.* Malden, MA: Blackwell, 1998.

Fowl, Stephen E., and L. Gregory Jones. *Reading in Communion: Scripture and Ethics in Christian Life.* Grand Rapids: Eerdmans, 1991.

————. "Scripture, Exegesis, and Discernment in Christian Ethics." In *Virtues and Practices in the Christian Tradition*, edited by Nancey Murphy, Brad J. Kallenberg, and Mark Thiessen Nation, 111–31. Harrisburg, PA: Trinity, 1997.

Franzelin, Johannes Baptist. *De Divina Traditione et Scriptura*. Rome: S. C. de Propag. Fide, 1870.

Freedmen, David Noel. "Headings in the Books of the Eight-Century Prophets." *Andrews University Seminary Studies* 25 (1987) 9–26.

Fretz, Mark J. H. "Lamentations and Literary Ethics: A New Perspective on Biblical Interpretation." PhD diss., University of Michigan, 1993.

Fuchs, Josef. *Christian Morality: The Word Becomes Flesh*. Translated by Brian McNeil. Washington, DC: Georgetown University Press, 1987.

Gadamer, Hans-Georg. "The Problem of Historical Consciousness." In *Interpretive Social Science*, edited by Paul Rabinow and William M. Sullivan, 82–140. Rev. ed. Berkeley: University of California Press, 1987.

Garcia-Treto, Francisco. "Crossing the Line." In *Teaching the Bible: The Discourses and Politics of Biblical Pedagogy*, edited by Fernando F. Segovia and Mary Ann Tolbert, 105–16. Maryknoll, NY: Orbis, 1998.

Gerstenberger, Erhard S. "Cultural Breaks, Cultural Conformity: The Case of Hermann Gunkel, Innovator of Exegetical Method." Paper presented at the Society of Biblical Literature International Meeting, Vienna, 2007.

————. *Theologies in the Old Testament*. Translated by John Bowden. Minneapolis: Fortress, 2002.

Gilkey, Langdon. "Cosmology, Ontology, and the Travail of Biblical Language." *JR* 61 (1961) 194–205.

Gonzalez-Gerth, Miguel. *A Labyrinth of Imagery: Ramón Gómez de la Serna's Novelas de la Nebulosa*. Colección Támesis. Serie A: Monografias 120. London: Tamesis, 1986.

Gorospe, Athena E. *Narrative and Identity: An Ethical Reading of Exodus 4*. BibIntSer 86. Leiden: Brill, 2007.

Green, Joel B. "The Bible, Theology, and Theological Interpretation." *SBL Forum*. September 2004. http://www.sbl–site.org/publications/article.aspx?ArticleId=308.

————. "Modernity, History, and the Theological Interpretation of the Bible." *SJT* 54 (2001) 308–29.

————. *Practicing Theological Interpretation: Engaging Biblical Texts for Faith and Formation*. Grand Rapids: Baker, 2011.

————. "Scripture and Theology: Failed Experiments, Fresh Perspectives." *Int* 56 (2002) 5–20.

Green, Joel B., and Tim Meadowcraft, eds. *Ears that Hear: Explorations in Theological Interpretation of the Bible*. Sheffield: Sheffield Phoenix, 2013.

Gregor, Brian. "Hermeneutics, Scripture, & Faithful Philosophizing: An Interview with Merold Westphal." *Journal of Philosphy and Scripture* 4.1 (2006) 26–40.

Gresch, Prosper. "Further Reflections on Biblical Inspiration and Truth." *BTB* 42 (2012) 81–89.

Grisez, Germain. *Beyond the New Theism: A Philosophy of Religion.* Notre Dame: Notre Dame University, 1975.

Grisez, Germain, and Joseph Boyle. "Responses to Our Critics and Our Collaborators." In *Natural Law and Moral Inquiry: Ethics, Metaphysics, and Politics in the Work of Germain Grisez,* edited by Robert P. George, 213–38. Washington, DC: Georgetown University Press, 1998.

Gruber, Margareta. "Quelle zu Trinken Geben." In *Bibelkanon in der Bibelauslegung: Methodenreflexionen und Beispielexegesen,* edited by Georg Stein and Egbert Ballhorn, 314–30. Stuttgart: Kohlhammer, 2007.

Gula, Richard M. *Reason Informed by Faith: Foundations of Catholic Morality.* New York: Paulist, 1989.

Gunkel, Hermann. *Water for a Thirsty Land: Israelite Literature and Religion.* Edited by K. C. Hanson. Translated by A. K. Dalles and James Schaaf. Fortress Classics in Biblical Studies. Minneapolis: Fortress, 2001.

Gutiérrez, Gustavo. *The God of Life.* Translated by Matthew J. O'Connell. Maryknoll, NY: Orbis, 1991.

Güttgemanns, Erhardt. *Candid Questions Concerning Gospel Form Criticism: A Methodological Sketch of the Fundamental Problematics of Form and Redaction Criticism.* Translated by William G. Doty. Pittsburgh Theological Monograph Series 26. Pittsburgh: Pickwick, 1970.

Habets, Myk. "'The Dogma is the Drama': Dramatic Developments in Biblical Theology." *Stimulus* 16.4 (2008) 1–4.

Hahn, Scott. *A Father Who Keeps His Promises: God's Covenant Love in Scripture.* Ann Arbor, MI: Charis, 1998.

———. "For the Sake of Our Salvation: The Truth and Humility of God's Word." *Letter & Spirit* 6 (2010) 21–45.

Hahn, Scott Walker, and John Sietze Bergsma. "What Laws Were 'Not Good'? A Canonical Approach to the Theological Problem of Ezekiel 20:25-26." *JBL* 123 (2004) 202–11.

Hahn, Scott W., and Benjamin Wiker. *Politicizing the Bible: The Roots of Historical Criticism and the Secularization of Scripture, 1300–1700.* New York: Crossroad, 2013.

Häring, Bernard. *Free and Faithful in Christ: Moral Theology for Clergy and Laity.* Vol. 1, *General Moral Theology.* New York: Seabury, 1978.

Harkins, Angela, K. "What Do Syriac/Antiochene Exegesis and Textual Criticism Have to Do with Theology?" In *Syrian & Antiochian Exegesis and Biblical Theology of the 3rd Millennium,* edited by Robert D. Miller II, 151–88. Piscataway, NJ: Gorgias, 2007.

Harrington, Daniel J. *Interpreting the Old Testament: A Practical Guide.* Old Testament Message 1. Wilmington, DE: Michael Glazier, 1981.

Harrington, Daniel J., and James F. Keenan. *Jesus and Virtue Ethics: Building Bridges between New Testament Studies and Moral Theology.* Lanham, MD: Sheed & Ward, 2002.

Harrington, Wilfred. "The Word of God." *ITQ* 29 (1962) 4–24.

Harrison, Brian W. "Restricted Inerrancy and the 'Hermeneutic of Discontinuity.'" *Letter & Spirit* 6 (2010) 225–46.

Hauerwas, Stanely. *Unleashing the Scripture: Freeing the Bible from Captivity to America.* Nashville: Abingdon, 1993.

———. "The Moral Authority of Scripture." In *The Use of Scripture in Moral Theology*, edited by Charles E. Curran and Richard A. McCormick, 242–75. Readings in Moral Theology 4. New York: Paulist, 1984.

Hayes, John H. "Wellhausen as a Historian of Israel." *Semeia* 25 (1983) 37–60.

Hays, Richard B. *The Moral Vision of the New Testament: Community, Cross, New Creation: A Contemporary Introduction to New Testament Ethics.* San Francisco: HarperSanFrancisco, 1996.

Healy, Mary. "Behind, in Front of . . . , or Through the Text? The Christological Analogy and the Lost World of Biblical Truth." In *Behind the Text: History and Biblical Interpretation*, edited by Craig Bartholomew et al., 181–95. Scripture and Hermeneutics Series 4. Grand Rapids: Eerdmans, 2003.

———. "Inspiration and Incarnation." *Letter & Spirit* 2 (2006) 27–42.

Hellwig, Monika K. "Bible and Interpretation." In *Biblical Studies: Meeting Ground of Jews and Christians*, edited by Lawrence Boadt et al., 172–98. Studies in Judaism and Christianity. New York: Paulist, 1981.

Helmer, Christine. "Biblical Theology: Bridge over Many Waters." *Currents in Biblical Research* 3 (2005) 169–96.

———. "'Open Systems': Constructive Philosophical and Theological Issues in Biblical Theology." *SBL Forum* September 2004. http://www.sbl-site.org/Article.aspx?ArticleId=310.

Heskett, Randall. "Deuteronomy 29–34 and the Formation of the Torah." In *The Bible as a Human Witness to Divine Revelation: Hearing the Word of God through Historically Dissimilar Traditions*, edited by Randall Heskett and Brian Irwin, 32–50. LHBOTS 469. London: Continuum, 2010.

———. *Messianism within the Scriptural Scrolls of Isaiah.* LHBOTS 456. London: T. & T. Clark, 2007.

Hetzenauer, Michael. *Wesen un Principien der Bibelkritik.* Innsbruck: Wagner, 1900.

House, Paul R. "God's Design and Postmodernism: Recent Approaches to Old Testament Theology." In *The Old Testament in the Life of God's People: Essays in Honor of Elmer A. Martens*, edited by Jon Isaak, 29–54. Winona Lake, IN: Eisenbrauns, 2009.

Huning, Ralf. "Between Text, Life Situation and Faith: Biblical Studies and Biblical Pastoral Ministry." *Bulletin Dei Verbum* 82/83 (2007) 8–11.

John Paul II, Pope. Address to the Pontifical Academy of Sciences, October 3, 1981.

Jackson, Pamela. "Cyril of Jerusalem's Use of Scripture." *TS* 52 (1991) 431–50.

Jeanrond, Werner G. *Text and Interpretation as Categories of Theological Thinking.* Translated by Thomas J. Wilson. New York: Crossroad, 1988.

———. *Theological Hermeneutics: Development and Significance*. New York: Crossroad, 1991.

Jensen, Alexander S. *Theological Hermeneutics*. London: SCM, 2007.

Johnson, Luke Timothy. *The Living Gospel*. New York: Continuum, 2004.

———. *The Real Jesus: The Misguided Quest for the Historical Jesus and the Truth of the Traditional Gospels*. San Francisco: HarperSanFrancisco, 1996.

———. "What's Catholic about Catholic Biblical Scholarship? An Opening Statement." In *The Future of Catholic Biblical Scholarship: A Constructive Conversation*, edited by Luke Timothy Johnson and William S. Kurz, 3–35. Grand Rapids: Eerdmans, 2002.

Joyce, Paul. "First among Equals: The Historical–Critical Approach in the Marketplace of Methods." In *Crossing the Boundaries: Essays in Biblical Interpretation in Honour of Michael D. Goulder*, edited by Stanley E. Porter et al., 17–27. BibIntSer 8. Leiden: Brill, 1994.

———. "Proverbs 8 in Interpretation." In *Reading Texts, Seeking Wisdom: Scripture and Theology*, edited by David F. Ford and Graham Stanton, 89–101. Grand Rapids: Eerdmans, 2004.

Kasper, Walter. "'*Dei Verbum* Audiens et Proclamans'—Hearing the Word of God with Reverence and Proclaiming It with Faith." Address to the Internation Congress "Sacred Scripture in the Life of the Church: 40th Anniversary of *Dei Verbum*." Rome, 2005.

Kelly, George A. "A Wayward Turn in Biblical Theory." *Catholic Dossier* (Jan/Feb 2000) 38–42.

Kelsey, David H. "Theological Use of Scripture in Process Hermeneutics." (1986) 181–88.

Kerbs, Raul. "Metodo Historico–Critico en Teologia." *Davar Logos* 2 (2000) 108–15.

Klein, Ralph W. "The Brevard Childs Proposal." *Word & World* 1 (1981) 105–15.

Knapp, Steven. "Collective Memory and the Actual Past." *Representations* 26 (1989) 123–49.

Koch, Klaus. *Was Ist Formgeschichte?* 1st ed. Neukirchen-Vluyn: Neukirchener, 1964.

———. *The Growth of the Biblical Tradition: The Form-Critical Method*. Translated by S. M. Cupitt. Scribner Studies in Biblical Interpretation. New York: Scribner, 1969.

Krisper, Crescentius. *Theologia Scholae Scotisticae*. Liege, 1729.

Kropf, Richard W. *Teilhard, Scripture, and Revelation: A Study of Teilhard de Chardin's Reinterpretation of Pauline Themes*. Rutherford, NJ: Fairleigh Dickenson University Press, 1980.

Kuhn, Johannes. "Zur Lehre von dem Worte Gottes und den Sacramenten." *TQ* 37 (1855) 3–57.

Kutsko, John F. "History as Liturgy and the Origins of the Lectionary." Paper presented at Duke Divinity School, Durham, NC, 2000.

Lagrange, Marie-Josèph. *Historical Criticism and the Old Testament*. 2nd ed. Translated by Edward Myers. London: Catholic Truth Society, 1906.

————. "Une Pensée de Saint Thomas sur l'inspiration scripturaire." *Revue Biblique* 4 (1895) 563–71.

————. "Les sources du troisime Evangile." *Revue Biblique* 5 (1896) 5–38.

Lambrecht, Jan. "*Dei Verbum* Forty Years Later." 40th Anniversary of Dei Verbum Lecture of the Irish Biblical Association, Dublin, 2005.

La Potterie, Ignace de. "Biblical Exegesis: A Science of Faith." In *Opening Up the Scriptures: Joseph Ratzinger and the Foundations of Biblical Interpretation*, edited by José Granados et al., 30–64. Grand Rapids: Eerdmans, 2008.

————. *The Hour of Jesus: The Passion and the Resurrection of Jesus according to John: Text and Spirit*. Translated by Gregory Murray. New York: Alba House, 1989.

————. "The Spiritual Sense of Scripture." *Communio* 23 (1996) 738–56.

Lategan, Bernard C. "Reader Response Theory." In *ABD* 5:627.

Latourelle, René. *Theology of Revelation: Including a Commentary on the Constitution "Dei verbum" of Vatican II*. 1966. Reprinted, Eugene, OR: Wipf & Stock, 2009.

Laurentin, René. *Evangiles de l'Enfance du Christ*. 2nd ed. Paris: Desclee, 1983.

————. *The Truth of Christmas beyond the Myths: The Gospels of the Infancy of Christ*. Translated by Michael J. Wrenn. Petersham, MA: St. Bede's, 1986.

Law, Timothy Michael. *When God Spoke Greek: The Septuagint and the Making of the Christian Bible*. Oxford: Oxford University Press, 2013.

Legrand, Lucien. "Fundamentalism and the Bible." *Bulletin Dei Verbum* 70/71 (2004) 9–15.

Lemke, Wener E. "Revelation through History in Recent Theology." *Int* 36 (1982) 34–46.

Levering, Matthew. *Engaging the Doctrine of Revelation: The Mediation of the Gospel through Church and Scripture*. Grand Rapids: Baker Academic, 2014.

Lewis, C. S. *The Weight of Glory, and Other Addresses*. New York: Macmillian, 1949.

Lindbeck, George. "The Search for Habitable Texts." *Daedalus* 117 (1988) 153–56.

————. "The Story-Shaped Church." In *Theological Interpretation of Scripture*, 39–52. Oxford: Blackwell, 1997.

Linkon, Sherry. "The Reader's Apprentice: Making Critical Cultural Reading Visible." *Pedagogy: Critical Approaches to Teaching Literature, Language, Composition, and Culture* 5 (2005) 247–73.

Lohfink, Norbert. "Alttestamentliche Wissenschaft als Theologie." In *Wieviel Systematik erlaubt die Schrift? Auf der Suche nach einer gesamtbiblischen Theologie*, edited by Frank-Lothar Hossfeld, 13–54. QD 185. Freiburg: Herder, 2001.

————. "*Über die Irrtumslosigk*eit und die Einheit der Schrift." *StZ* 174 (1964) 161–81.

Lubac, Henri de. *Catholicisme: Les aspects sociaux du Dogma Chretien*. Rev. ed. Traditions chrétiennes 13. Paris: Cerf, 1941. Reprinted, 1983.

Lundhaug, Hugo. "Canon and Interpretation: A Cognitive Perspective." In *Canon and Canonicity*, edited by Einarr Thomassen, 71–86. Copenhagen: Museum Tusculanum, 2010.

Machinist, Peter. "William Foxwell Albright: The Man and His Work." In *The Study of the Ancient Near East in the Twenty-First Century*, edited by Jerrold S. Cooper and Glenn M. Schwartz, 385–404. Winona Lake, IN: Eisenbrauns, 1996.

Martin, Francis. "Literary Theory, Philosophy of History and Exegesis." *The Thomist* 52 (1988) 575–604.

————. "Some Directions in Catholic Biblical Theology." In *Out of Egypt: Biblical Theology and Biblical Interpretation*, edited by Craig Bartholomew et al., 65–87. Grand Rapids: Zondervan, 2004.

————. "Spirit and Flesh in the Doing of Theology." *Journal of Pentecostal Theology* 18 (2001) 5–31.

————. "The Word at Prayer: Epistemology in the Psalms." In *The Bible and Epistemology: Biblical Soundings on the Knowledge of God*, edited by Mary Healy and Robin Parry, 43–64. Milton Keynes, UK: Paternoster, 2007.

Mason, Rex. "H. Wheeler Robinson Revisited." *Baptist Quarterly* 37 (1998) 213–26.

Matera, Frank. "New Testament Theology." *CBQ* 67 (2005) 1–21.

Matthews, Susan F. "When We Remembered Zion." In *The Bible on Suffering: Social and Political Implications*, edited by Anthony J. Tambasco, 93–119. New York: Paulist, 2002.

McCambly, Richard. "Notes on the Song of Songs." http://www.bhsu.edu/artssciences/asfaculty/dsalomon/ld/songnotes.html.

McCarthy, Dennis J. "God as Prisoner of Our Own Choosing: Critical-Historical Study of the Bible." In *Historicism and Faith: Proceedings of the Fellowship of Catholic Scholars*, edited by Paul L. Williams, 17–47. Scranton, PA: Northeast Books, 1980.

McCarthy, David Matzko. "Catholic Social Thought." Proceedings of the Fourth Annual Lilly Fellows National Research Conference, Stamford, CT, 2004.

McDonald, Patricia. "Biblical Scholarship: When Tradition Met Method." In *The Catholic Church in the Twentieth Century*, edited by John Deedy, 113–30. Collegeville, MN: Liturgical, 2000.

————. *God and Violence: Biblical Resources for Living in a Small World*. Scottdale, PA: Herald, 2004.

McGowan, Michael. *The Bridge: Revelation and Its Implications*. Eugene, OR: Pickwick, 2015.

McKenzie, John L. *Myths and Realities: Studies in Biblical Theology*. 1963. Reprinted, Eugene, OR: Wipf & Stock, 2009.

McKnight, Edgar V. "Reader-Response Criticism." In *To Each Its Own Meaning: An Introduction to Biblical Criticisms and Their Application*, edited by Stephen R. Haynes and Steven L. McKenzie, 230–52. Louisville: Westminster John Knox, 1993.

McLean, B. H. *Biblical Interpretation and Philosophical Hermeneutics.* New York: Cambridge University Press, 2012.

Metz, Johannes Baptist. "A Short Apology of Narrative." *Concilium* 85 (1975) 84–96.

Meynet, Roland. "Two Decalogues: Law of Freedom." *Studia Rhetorica* 16 (2004) 1–35.

Middleton, J. Richard. *The Liberating Image: The Imago Dei in Genesis 1.* Grand Rapids: Brazos, 2005.

Miller, Patrick D. *The Way of the Lord: Essays in Old Testament Theology.* FAT 39. Tübingen: Mohr/Siebeck, 2004.

Miller, Robert D., II, ed. *Between Israelite Religion and Biblical Theology.* Contributions to Biblical Exegesis and Theology 80. Leuven: Peeters, 2016.

———. *Oral Tradition in the Old Testament.* Biblical Performance Criticism Series 4. Eugene, OR: Cascade Books, 2011.

Miskotte, Kornelis. "Bijbels ABC." In *Kornelis Miskotte: A Biblical Theology.* Translated by Martin Kessler. Selinsgrove: Susquehanna University Press, 1997.

———. *Zur biblischen Hermeneutik.* Translated by Hinrich Stoevesant. ThSt 55. Zollikon: Evangelischer Verlag, 1959.

Möller, Karl. "Reconstructing and Interpreting Amos's Literary Prehistory: A Dialogue with Redaction Criticism." In *Behind the Text: History and Biblical Interpretation,* edited by Craig Bartholomew et al., 397–442. Grand Rapids: Zondervan, 2003.

Moller, Philip. "What Should They Be Saying about Biblical Interpretation?" *TS* 74 (2013) 605–31.

Montagnes, Bernard. *The Story of Father Marie-Joseph Lagrange: Founder of Modern Catholic Bible Study.* Translated by Benedict Viviano. Mahwah, NJ: Paulist, 2005.

Moore, Stephen D., and Yvonne Sherwood. "Biblical Studies 'after' Theory: Onwards towards the Past, Part Two; The Secret Vices of the Biblical God." *BibInt* 18 (2010) 87–113.

Morrow, Jeffrey. "The Politics of Biblical Interpretation." *New Blackfriars* 91 (2010) 528–45.

Mosala, Itumeleng. *Biblical Hermeneutics and Black Theology in South Africa.* Grand Rapids: Eerdmans, 1989.

Mowinckel, Sigmund. *The Old Testament as Word of God: Its Significance for a Living Christian Faith.* Translated by R. B. Bjornard. New York: Abingdon, 1959.

Murphy, Austin. "*Dei Verbum*, St. Augustine, and Modernity on Biblical Inspiration." Paper presented at the conference "Dei Verbum at 50: Toward a Clarification of the Inspiration of Scripture. Dayton, 2012.

Murphy-O'Connor, Jerome. "1 Corinthians 11:2–16 Once Again." *CBQ* 50 (1988) 265–74.

———. "Interpolation in 1 Corinthians 11:2–16." *CBQ* 48 (1986) 81–94.

———. "Sex and Logic in 1 Corinthians 11:2–16." *CBQ* 42 (1980) 482–500.

Murphy, Roland E. *Experiencing our Biblical Heritage.* Peabody, MA: Hendrickson, 2001.

———. "When Is Theology Biblical?" Paper presented at "Washington Theological Union Evening Scholars' Conversation." Washington, DC, 2001.

Newman, John Henry. "On the Inspiration of Scripture." *The Nineteenth Century* 15.84 (1884) 185–99.

Norris, Thomas. "On Revisiting *Dei Verbum.*" *ITQ* 66 (2001) 315–37.

Nürnberger, Klaus. *Biblical Theology in Outline: The Vitality of the Word of God.* Pietermaritzburg: Cluster, 2004.

———. "On Biblical Interpretation: Evolutionary Hermeneutics—A Position Paper." http://www.klaus-nurnberger.com/images/stories/new_pdf_docs/position_papers/pos-pap-hermeneutics.pdf.

———. *Theology of the Biblical Witness: An Evolutionary Approach.* Theologie, Forschung und Wissenschaft 5. Münster: LIT, 2002.

Ochs, Peter. "Scriptural Logic." In *Rethinking Metaphysics*, edited by Gregory Jones and Stephen E. Fowl, 62–95. Directions in Modern Theology. Cambridge, MA: Blackwell, 1995.

O'Keefe, John J. "Rejecting One's Masters: Theodoret of Cyrus, Antiochene Exegesis, and the Patristic Mainstream." In *Syriac and Antiochian Exegesis and Biblical Theology of the 3rd Millennium*, edited by Robert D. Miller, 243–64. Gorgias Eastern Christian Studies 6. Piscataway, NJ: Gorgias, 2007.

Osiek, Carolyn. "Catholic or catholic? Biblical Scholarship at the Center." *JBL* 125 (2006) 5–22.

———. "The Family in Early Christianity." *CBQ* 58 (1996) 1–24.

Paglia, Vincenzo. *La Bibbia Ridona il Cuore.* Milan: Leonardo International, 2005.

Pallesen, Carsten. "Philosophy of Reflection and Biblical Revelation in Paul Ricoeur." *ST* 62 (2008) 44–62.

Pannenberg, Wolfhart. *Basic Questions in Theology.* 3 vols. Translated by George H. Kehm and R. A. Wilson. Philadelphia: Fortress, 1970.

Pegues, R. P. Thomas. *Catechism of the "Summa Theologica" of Saint Thomas Aquinas for the Use of the Faithful.* Translated by Aelred Whitacre. New York: Benziger, 1922.

Perdue, Leo G. *The Collapse of History.* Overtures to Biblical Theology. Minneapolis: Fortress, 1994.

Peterson, David L. "Review of Seitz's Prophecy and Hermeneutics." Paper Presented at Society of Biblical Literature Annual Meeting, San Diego, 2007.

Pidel, Aaron. "Social Inspiration According to Joseph Ratzinger." Paper presented at the conference "*Dei Verbum* at 50: Toward a Clarification of the Inspiration of Scripture." Dayton, 2012.

Pinckaers, Servais. *Morality: The Catholic View.* Translated by Michael Sherwin. South Bend, IN: St. Augustine's, 2001.

Pitre, Brant. "The Mystery of God's Word: Inspiration, Inerrancy, and the Interpretation of Scripture." *Letter & Spirit* 6 (2010) 47–66.

Poirier, John C. "The Canonical Approach and the Idea of 'Scripture.'" *ExpTim* 11 (2005) 366–70.

Pregeant, Russell. *Christology beyond Dogma: Matthew's Christ in Process Hermeneutic.* Semeia Supplements 7. Philadelphia: Fortres, 1978.

Preuss, Horst Dietrich. *Old Testament Theology.* Vol. 2. Translated by Leo G. Perdue. OTL. Louisville: Westminster John Knox, 1996.

Prior, Joseph G. *The Historical Critical Method in Catholic Exegesis.* Tesi Gregoriana, Serie Theologia 50. Rome: Gregorian Pontifical University Press, 1999.

Pythian-Adams, W. J. "Shadow and Substance: The Meaning of Sacred History." *Int* 1 (1947) 419–35.

Rad, Gerhard von. *Biblical Interpretations in Preaching.* John E. Steely. Nashville: Abingdon, 1977.

———. *God at Work in Israel.* Translated by John H. Marks. Nashville: Abingdon, 1980.

———. *Old Testament Theology.* 2 vols. Translated by D. M. G. Stalker. New York: Harper & Row, 1962, 1965.

Rae, Murray A. *History and Hermeneutics.* New York: T. & T. Clark, 2005.

———. "Texts in Context: Scripture and the Divine Economy." *JTI* 1 (2007) 23–45.

Rahner, Karl. "Exegesis and Dogmatic Theology." In *Theological Investigations,* 5:67–93. Translated by Karl-H. Kruger. London: Dartman, Longman & Todd, 1966.

———. *Grundkurs des Glauben: Einführung in den Begriff des Christentums.* 5th ed. Freiburg: Herder, 1976.

———. "Observations on the Concept of Revelation." In *Revelation and Tradition,* by Karl Rahner and Joseph Ratzinger, 9–25. Translated by W. J. O'Hara. Quaestiones disputatae 17. New York: Herder & Herder, 1966.

Räisänen, Heikki. "The Effective 'History' of the Bible." *SJT* 45 (1992) 303–24.

———. *Beyond New Testament Theology: A Story and a Programme.* Philadelphia: Trinity, 1990.

Ratzinger, Joseph. "Biblical Interpretation in Crisis: On the Question of the Foundations and Approaches of Exegesis Today." In *Biblical Interpretation in Crisis,* edited by Richard J. Neuhaus, 1–23. Grand Rapids: Eerdmans, 1989.

———. "The Dogmatic Constitution on Divine Revelation: A Commentary." *Bulletin Dei Verbum* (2005) 4.

———. *God and the World: A Conversation with Peter Seewald.* San Francisco: Ignatius, 2000.

———. *Jesus of Nazareth: From the Baptism in the Jordan to the Transfiguration.* Translated by Adrian J. Walker. New York: Doubleday, 2007.

———. "Revelation and Tradition." In *Revelation and Tradition,* by Karl Rahner and Joseph Ratzinger, 25–49. QD 17. New York: Herder & Herder, 1966.

Rendtorff, Rolf. *The Canonical Hebrew Bible: A Theology of the Old Testament.* Tools for Biblical Study 7. Leiden: Deo, 2005.

———. "Canonical Interpretation." *Pro Ecclesia* 3 (1994) 141–51.

———. "'Covenant' as Structuring Concept in Genesis and Exodus." *JBL* 108 (1989) 385–93.

———. "Gerhard von Rad's Contribution to Biblical Studies." In *Proceedings of the Sixth World Congress of Jew Studies*, 350–56. Jerusalem: World Union of Jewish Studies, 1977.

———. "The Paradigm is Changing: Hopes—and Fears." *BibInt* 1 (1992) 34–53.

Reno, Russell R. "Biblical Theology and Theological Exegesis." In *Behind the Text: History and Biblical Interpretation*, edited by Craig Bartholomew et al., 385–408. Grand Rapids: Eerdmans, 2003.

Reusch, Franz Heinrich. *Lehrbuch der Einleitung in das Alte Testament.* Freiburg: Herder, 1870.

Robinson, Robert Bruce. "Narrative Theology and Biblical Theology." In *The Promise and Practice of Biblical Theology*, edited by John Reumann, 129–42. Philadelphia: Fortress, 1991.

———. *Roman Catholic Exegesis since Divino Afflante Spiritu.* SBL Dissertation Series 111. Atlanta: Scholars, 1988.

Rousseau, Philip. *The Early Christian Centuries.* London: Longman, 2002.

Ruotolo, Dolindo. *La Sacra Scrittura: Psicologia–Commento–Meditazione.* 9 vols. Gravina di Puglia: Seminario Vescoville, 1930–39.

———. *Un gravissimo pericolo per la Chiesa e per le anima.* Naples: n.p., 1941.

Ryan, Stephen D. "The Word of God and the Textual Pluriformity of the Old Testament." http://www.stthomas.edu/spssod/pdf/quinn/Ryan_Word_of_God_%20Fi.pdf.

Sanders, James A. "Scripture as Canon for Post-Modern Times." *BTB* 25 (1995) 56–63.

———. *Torah and Canon.* 2nd ed. Eugene, OR: Cascade Books, 2005.

Sargent, Benjamin. "John Milbank and Biblical Hermeneutics: The End of the Historical–Critical Method?" *Heythrop Journal* 53 (2012) 253–63.

Sarisky, Darren. *Scriptural Interpretation.* Challenges in Contemporary Theology. Malden, MA: Wiley, 2013.

Scheffczyk, Leo. "Biblische und Dogmatische Theologie." *TTZ* 67 (1958) 193–209.

———. "Sacred Scripture: God's Word and The Church's Word." *Communio* 28 (2001) 26–41.

Schenker, Adrian. "Die Heilige Schrift subsistiert gleichzeitig in mehreren kanonischen Formen." In *Studien zu Propheten und Religionsgeschichte*, 192–200. Stuttgarter biblische Aufsatzbände 36. Stuttgart: Katholisches Bibelwerk, 2003.

Schillebeeckx, Edward. *Christ: The Experience of Jesus as Lord.* Translated by John Bowden. New York: Seabury, 1980.

———. *Church: The Human Story of God.* Translated by John Bowden. New York: Seabury, 1990.

————. *Revelation and Theology.* Vol. 1. Translated by N. D. Smith. New York: Sheed & Ward, 1967.

Schneiders, Sandra M. *The Revelatory Text: Interpreting the New Testament as Sacred Scripture.* New York: HarperCollins, 1991.

Schroeder, Francis J. *Père Lagrange and Biblical Inspiration.* Catholic University of America Studies in Sacred Theology 2/80. Washington, DC: Catholic University of America Press, 1954.

Scullion, James. "The Writings of Francis and the Gospel of John." Paper presented at Washington Theological Union Symposium on Franciscans and the Scriptures, Washington, DC, 2005.

Seitz, Christopher R. *The Character of Christian Scripture: The Significance of a Two-Testament Bible.* Studies in Theological Interpretation. Grand Rapids: Baker, 2011.

————. *The Goodly Fellowship of the Prophets: The Achievement of Association in Canon Formation.* Acadia Studies in Bible and Theology. Grand Rapids: Baker, 2009.

————. "On Letting a Text 'Act like a Man.'" *Scottish Bulletin of Evangelical Theology* 22 (2004) 159–72.

————. *Prophecy and Hermeneutics: Toward a New Introduction to the Prophets.* Studies in Theological Interpretation. Grand Rapids: Baker Academic, 2007.

Semmelroth, Otto. "Heilige Schrift als Glaubensquelle." *StZ* 161 (1958) 36–49.

Sheppard, Gerald T. "The Book of Isaiah as a Human Witness to Revelation within the Religions of Judaism and Christianity." In *SBLSP,* 274–80. Atlanta: Scholars, 1993.

————. "Canonical Criticism." In *ABD* 1:861–66.

————. "Canonization: Hearing the Voice of the Same God through Historically Dissimilar Traditions." *ExAud* 1 (1985) 21–33.

Simian-Yofre, Horacio. "Old and New Testament: Participation and Analogy." In *Vatican II: Assessment and Perspectives: Twenty-five Years after (1962–1987),* edited by René Latourelle, vol. 1, pt. 2:267–98. 3 vols. in 7 parts. New York: Paulist, 1988.

Sláma, Petr. "Beyond, Before and Within the Text of the Bible." Paper presented to the Society of Biblical Literature International Meeting, Vienna, 2007.

Smith, Mark S. *God in Translation: Deities in Cross-Cultural Discourse in the Biblical World.* FAT 57. Tübingen: Mohr/Siebeck, 2008.

————. *The Memoirs of God: History, Memory, and the Experience of the Divine in Ancient Israel.* Minneapolis: Fortress, 2004.

————. "Monotheistic Re–Readings of the Biblical God." *RelSRev* 27.1 (2001) 25–31.

Sonnet, J. P. "Inscrire le nouveau dans l'ancien." *NRTh* 128 (2006) 3–17.

Spawn, K. L., and Archie T. Wright. *Spirit and Scripture: Exploring a Pneumatic Hermeneutic.* London: Continuum, 2011.

Spohn, William C. *What Are They Saying about Scripture and Ethics?* Rev. ed. New York: Paulist, 1995.

Steinmetz, David. "The Superiority of Pre-Critical Exegesis." *ThTo* 37 (1980) 27–38.

Stendahl, Krister. *Meanings: The Bible as Document and as Guide.* Philadelphia: Fortress, 1984.

Stevenson, W. Taylor. "Myth and the Crisis of Historical Consciousness." In *Myth and the Crisis of Historical Consciousness,* edited by Lee W. Gibbs and W. Taylor Stevenson, 1–17. Missoula, MT: Scholars, 1975.

Stolze, Radegundis. *The Translator's Approach: Introduction to Translational Hermeneutics: Theory and Examples from Practice.* Arbeiten zur Theorie und Praxis des Überstezens und Dolmetschens 41. Berlin: Frank & Timme, 2011.

Strecker, Georg. *Theology of the New Testament.* Edited and completed by Friedrich Wilhelm Horn. Translated by M. Eugene Boring. Louisville: Westminster John Knox, 2000.

Sweeney, Marvin L. "Review of Seitz's *Prophecy and Hermeneutics.*" Paper presented at the Society of Biblical Literature Annual Meeting, San Diego, 2007.

Swinburne, Richard. *Revelation: From Metaphor to Analogy.* 2nd ed. Oxford: Oxford University Press, 2007.

Teilhard de Chardin, Pierre. *Hymn of the Universe.* Translated by Simon Bartholomew. New York: Harper & Row, 1965.

———. *Science and Christ.* Translated by René Hague. New York: Harper & Row, 1968.

Théobald, Christophe. "A quelles conditions une théologie 'biblique' de l'histoire est–elle aujourd'hui possible?" In *Comment la Bible saisit–elle l'histoire?,* edited by D. Doré, 266–74. Paris: Cerf, 2007.

Tilley, Robert. "The Birth of Ideology." *Crucible* 5.1 (May 2013) 1–22.

Tillich, Paul. *Biblical Religion and the Search for Ulitmate Reality.* Chicago: Chicago University Press, 1955.

Todorov, Tzvetan. "How to Read?" In *The Poetics of Prose,* 234–46. Translated by Richard Howard. Ithaca, NY: Cornell University Press, 1977.

Topel, John. "Faith, Exegesis, and Theology." *ITQ* 69 (2004) 337–48.

Tracy, David. *On Naming the Present: Reflections on God, Hermeneutics, and Church.* Concilium. Maryknoll, NY: Orbis, 1994.

Trembath, Kern. "Response to Professor Helmut Gabel's 'Inspiration and Truth of the Writing.'" In *L'Interpretazione della Bibbia nella Chiesa,* 85–89. Atti e Documenti 11. Rome: Vatican Library Press, 2001.

Trier, Daniel J. *Introducing Theological Interpretation of Scripture: Recovering a Christian Practice.* Grand Rapids: Baker, 2008.

Tucker, W. Dennis, Jr. "From Biblical Exegesis to Theological Construction." *SBL Forum* September 2004. http://www.sbl-site.org/publications/article.aspx?ArticleId=309.

Vall, Gregory. "Psalm 22: Vox Christi or Israelite Temple Liturgy?" *The Thomist* 66 (2002) 175–200.

Vaux, Roland de. "Is it Possible to Write a 'Theology of the Old Testament.'" In *The Bible and the Ancient Near East*, 49–62. Translated by Damian McHugh. Garden City, NJ: Doubleday & Company, 1971.

Vawter, Bruce. *Biblical Inspiration*. Theological Resources. Philadelphia: Westminster, 1972.

Verdes, Lorenzo Alvarez. "Ética Bíblica y Hermenéutica." *Studia Moralia* 35 (1997) 313–43.

Walsh, Carey. *Chasing Mystery: A Catholic Biblical Theology*. Collegeville, MN: Liturgical, 2012.

Wellhausen, Julius. *Prolegomena to the History of Ancient Israel*. 1878. Reprinted, New York: Meridian, 1957.

Wénin, André. "Analyse narrative et théologie dans le récit biblique." In *Aujourd'hui, lire la Bible*, edited by Philippe Abadie, 48–56. Paris: Profac, 2008.

White, Wesley. *Hermeneutical and Exegetical Reflections on Isaiah 58:1–12.* Scottish Universities Theological Forum, 2005.

Wicks, Jared. "Six Texts by Prof. Joseph Ratzinger as Peritus before and during Vatican II." *Gregorianum* 89 (2008) 233–311.

Wilken, Robert Louis. "The Bishop as Exegete: Interpreting Scripture by Scripture." Presentation to the United States Conference of Catholic Bishops on the 40th Anniversary of *Dei Verbum*, Chicago, 2005.

Williams, David. *Receiving the Bible in Faith: Historical and Theological Exegesis.* Washington, DC: Catholic University of America Press, 2004.

Williamson, Peter. *Catholic Principles for Interpreting Scripture: A Study of the Pontifical Biblical Commission's The Interpretation of the Bible in the Church.* Subsidiea Biblica 22. Rome: Pontifical Biblical Institute Press, 2001.

———. "Catholic Principles for Interpreting Scripture." Paper presented to the Catholic Biblical Association Annual Meeting, Cleveland, 2002.

Wisse, Maarten. "Narrative Theology and the Use of the Bible in Systematic Theology." *Ars Disputandi* 5 (2005) http://www.arsdisputandi.org.

Wojtyla, Karol. *Sources of Renewal: The Implementation of the Second Vatican Council.* Translated by P. S. Falla. San Francisco: Harper & Row, 1980.

Wolterstorff, Nicholas. *Divine Discourse: Philosophical Reflections on the Claim that God Speaks.* Cambridge: Cambridge University Press, 1995.

Wright, G. Ernest. *God Who Acts.* Studies in Biblical Theology 8. London: SCM, 1952.

Wright, G. Ernest, and Reginald H. Fuller. *The Book fo the Acts of God.* London: Duckworth, 1960.

Zenger, Erich. "'Gott hat keiner jemals geschaut' (Joh 1, 18) Die christliche Gottesrede im Angesicht des Judentums." July 2005. http://ivv7srv15. uni-muenster.de/zrat/Abschiedsvorlesung%2014.%20Juli%202004%20 Kurzfassung.doc.

Index